PLANET A

A Mother's Memoir of Autism Spectrum Disorder

Diane Mayer Christiansen

ISBN: 0692792023
ISBN 13: 9780692792025
Library of Congress Control Number: 2016918437
Diane Mayer Christiansen, Glenview, ILLINOIS

This book is dedicated to all those touched by autism spectrum disorder.
And to Alexander and Jackie for their courage and honesty.

A huge thank you to those special few who worked their magic in the editing process: Kurt Christiansen (Uncle Kurt), Grandma and Grandpa Mayer, and Mrs. Marilyn Parolini. Your input has been a vital part of the process.

PREFACE

My son, Jackie, plays basketball, which is a good thing since he's fourteen years old and six foot two. He towers over the other eighth graders, and I feel a bit sorry for the five-foot offensive player whom he's guarding most of the time. Jackie can hit a three pointer, and his passing is pretty good, but he has difficulty being aggressive under the hoop. Actually, he has trouble being aggressive anywhere. He doesn't like that kind of physical contact. I can't say I blame him.

After a particularly hard loss, I watched as the players lined up to shake hands; Jackie's head hung low in defeat. Winning is everything to him. Sitting in the crowded stands, I readied myself to begin the *winning isn't everything* and *you did a good job* speeches. As he looked up to me, I gave him an encouraging smile, and in return, he flipped me the bird! I had to look twice to really comprehend the gesture. Yes, it was definitely the middle finger. I glanced behind my shoulder to where a mother sat with her four-year-old daughter, and I began the apologies.

"I'm so sorry about that. My son has autism, and he is very reactive. He doesn't always think before he acts." The people around me were nice, but I couldn't help think about how unfair it was for those innocent bystanders. Yeah, it's just the middle finger and, yeah, maybe no one really saw it, but still. Of course, Jackie and I had a long talk once he cooled down, and I haven't seen the gesture since, but I am constantly asking myself what is next. Believe me when I say there's always a next...and a next...and a next.

Autism has become a big part of my life, maybe the biggest part. The road that I began walking as a mother of an autistic child has twisted and turned over time. I have found myself stepping into the role of advocate, not only for kids with ASD (autism spectrum disorder) and special needs kids but also for all children. Speaking has been my greatest love: educating and sharing stories about my path with Jackie and teaching others to celebrate the things that make us different. Whenever I speak to groups about my journey, I always start with the same disclaimer: my name is Diane Mayer Christiansen, and I am not a pediatrician, a therapist, or a neurologist.

I'm just a mom. Of course, the truth is that ASD has made me a pediatrician, a therapist, and a neurologist, at least in my private life. Ever since my son Jackie's diagnosis back in the second grade, I've been forced into these roles, of searching out information and better ways to understand him and how his brain works differently than those in the typical world. From the day of that diagnosis, my life changed dramatically. I had to throw away all of the parenting ideas that I had embraced up until that moment. I had to modify my dreams for him. I had to begin the fight for others to understand him, a fight that continues today.

Over the years of advocating for Jackie, I have asked myself the same question: Am I using autism as a crutch even as I tell Jackie he cannot use it as an excuse? I worry about this. It seems as if I am constantly making every difficult situation center on autism and am always fighting against those who would try to fit a square peg into a round hole. I know how some people view me: making excuse after excuse and always with autism at the forefront. I have heard the comments: *maybe if you just stopped talking about ASD all the time, it wouldn't be such a big deal.* What if I just stopped advocating? Would he find a way to blend in? Would he be better off? Nevertheless, the question of crutch using and the push to stop talking about ASD is all wrapped into one big problem. Jackie has ASD, and it's a real neurological issue. He learns differently, relates to others differently, and handles internal struggles differently. The truth is that I never wanted to make Jackie's life about his autism. I never wanted him to be different, and I always hoped for a day when he would fit in. I think the biggest problem for me has been the inability of those around me—teachers, parents, and Jackie's peers—to truly understand how an ASD brain works. I went through the years hearing, *He's just like everyone else his age* and *all kids go through these stages.* In the beginning, I felt relief when I heard these words, but as time went on, I wondered why no one could see the differences. I worried that Jackie would be judged without a true understanding of where his behavior was coming from. I found myself explaining the low level of maturity that Jackie displayed and the inappropriate behaviors, all associated with ASD. I knew Jackie's ASD was not going anywhere. I now realize that I can't change the way other people see him or see his behavior. I hope that this book paves the way to open the minds of others. I hope that it helps others to see ASD in a new light and to accept it as a real, viable neurological difference, one that should be embraced with understanding and acceptance.

The brain is a funny machine. I know because dyslexia complicated my early learning experiences. My brain simply could not organize letters into words. I accomplished verbalization of thought with no less difficulty. Other kids could read aloud in class, but for me, the text appeared to be jumping off the page. For Jackie, it's kind of the same thing. His ASD brain misinterprets data from all of his sensory devices: sight, sound, taste, smell, and touch. Ordinary stimuli that do not tax a normal brain—a loud noise or a strange odor or taste—can disorient Jackie, sending him into a panic mode. Words, language, and their nuances may mislead or escape him, causing an immediate and inappropriate reply. In effect, his ASD brain causes him to exist on an alien planet. This is his brain. Think of it as a complex computer with information moving back and forth in a regular pattern. A signal comes to your brain that you are hungry. You reach for a banana. It is yellow and has a certain feel, smell, and taste. Your brain easily assimilates these variable stimuli, you eat the banana, and your hunger is satisfied. For Jackie, this complex of moving data is jammed. Too much information or stimuli move back and forth, clogging the system. Simultaneous data from multiple sensory sources may put his brain on overload causing confusion and dysfunction as a result. Perhaps smell is the sole stimulant to which his brain can respond, and that is highly amplified. All of the information is tied up in that one sense of smell, and it's concentrated to the point of being offensive. It's like a jolt of electricity, hitting the olfactory senses hard. That's how it works with all his senses. When he's finger painting, the sense of touch dominates, and the slimy paint may become repugnant. What he hears in a room filled with people he may interpret as indecipherable noise rather than a collection of individual conversations. A friend speaking in a soft modulated tone implying friendship may not be sure that the message communicated is always in Jackie's best interest. Because of this single stimuli phenomenon, he is also a black-and-white thinker with no room for gray. Many times, that in-between gray is an impossibility for him; it just doesn't exist. To Jackie, ASD is normal. He doesn't understand why his peers find fault with behavior that his brain portrays as logical and justified.

So, what is it like having a child with ASD, and what does it take to parent him? I can only tell you what I have gone though, what my personal experiences have been, and what I have learned from other moms, a few therapists, and doctors along the way. It hasn't been easy. It can be difficult for parents to work together. Since Jackie's father, Jack Sr., is the breadwinner, his focus has had to be on work. However, even as busy as he is, Jack has been the one to push Jackie at times when I wanted to be protective. When basketball season came around in sixth grade, I thought, *No, this won't be good.* I saw how the boys fought underneath the basket, vying for rebounds. Jack was there reminding me how important it was to let Jackie try things, and so I reluctantly agreed. Those years of basketball were invaluable. Yes, in the beginning, there were a few freak-outs about being touched, but Jackie loved the game. He learned how to work on a team, how to lose gracefully (sometimes), and how to build new relationships that have lasted. He and his father's trips to Monster Jam, the race track, and professional basketball games—all events that I worried would be too loud or too crowded—built memories and proved that once in a while, Jackie can handle being out of his comfort zone. Even though there are times that I wish more than anything that I could trade roles and go off to a job that would take me away from all of the crazy, those times are rare. And even though this book is about my journey with a son who has autism, his father has contributed greatly in an effort to help Jackie feel like he does fit in.

⇥ ⇤

My involvement in Jackie's caregiving has been all consuming most days. I am sure that Jack's story about living with ASD would look very different from mine. For me, the struggle has been with the dichotomy of advocating for my son while also trying to understand how the world around us sees his behavior. Educating myself has been the key. The minute that Jackie was diagnosed, my education began. I realized very quickly that not only did I need to be educated, but so did the world. I've had my share of dirty looks on the playground or in the grocery store. I've been called an enabler and made to feel like a bad mom. I've even been accused of allowing my son to be autistic. I also know that I'm not alone in this journey. If you are a parent of a child with ASD, I want you to know that you are not alone, either.

This is a book to share. I want to give everyone a glimpse into what ASD looks like from the inside, from a mom's and a fourteen-year-old ASD boy's points of view. Mostly, I want to show you how we celebrate it, how we take the negative and turn it around. It's not always easy...well, the truth is it's never easy, but being a parent is a tough job. So, I hope you'll come along for the ride. It's a bumpy one, but there's a lot of awesome stuff to discover on Planet Autism—Planet A.

CHAPTER ONE

When I picked up my son, Jackie, from school recently, I could tell by his face that it hadn't been a good day. Middle school had been a rough transition for him. He got into the car and began to cry. When I asked him what had happened he took a deep breath and told me that he was just tired of everyone telling him how annoying he was. I tried to make him feel better with kind words, but he stopped me and said:

> Mom, sometimes I feel like everyone but me lives on planet Earth and that it's great here. Everyone understands everyone else, and

most people are happy. But then I live on this other planet, Planet Autism. It's far away and maybe not as nice, and I'm all alone there. When you talk to groups about my autism, I feel like you're giving them directions to my planet, and that's good. The problem is that no one wants to visit because it's too far away, too much trouble to get to, and they're afraid that there's not going to be anything good there. So, in the end, I'm still all alone. I really wish I could get someone to visit.

Whoa, I thought, *that was really a profound idea.* And it made me so sad to think that Jackie felt so alone and so misunderstood.

"Well, I like Planet Autism, Planet A," I said. "And that's why we write books about it and why we talk to people about it." He nodded. "That's our mission, Jackie, to get people to understand what it's like for those on Planet A." He gave me a half smile, making me think that I was making progress in cheering him up. "You're having a bad day, but think about how many other ASD kids feel the same way. If we can get people to understand your planet, we will also be helping those kids. We'll be showing them all the cool stuff about your world, like your awesome photographic memory and your great sense of humor. And wouldn't it be great if Planet A wouldn't need to be a separate planet at all, but a part of Earth, a piece of what makes up the human race?" That got a full smile, but I could still see the sadness in his eyes. I wondered, then, if we would ever get anyone to visit. I wondered if we ever would get anyone to really understand. After everything that we had been through together, the hurt and the tears as well as the celebrations, why were we still here in this place of sadness? Looking back, I almost felt that the beginning had been easier. In the beginning, there was hope that he would eventually understand his peers, or at least that they would understand him. Back then, I think that ignorance was bliss—well, almost bliss.

Jackie was born around Christmastime, 2001. It was a difficult delivery. I won't get into the graphic details, but it ended in a C-section, and I was just happy to be alive. He had problems in the hospital: jaundice and feeding issues, but nothing alarming. I was completely oblivious to taking care of a baby, and my nerves were crazy. I asked the nurse a million questions until she finally stopped coming into my room. I made them show me repeatedly how to change his diaper and freaked out when they finally told me it was time to go home. Of course, as all new mothers do, I quickly got the hang of it. What choice did I have?

I'm a planner, a scientist by training, and I can always stick to the schedule as long as I have a list in front of me. So being a mother came easily after I learned how to get the diaper on so that it would stay. The early days were great, especially after the haze of the first three months was gone. By then, Jackie was sleeping eight hours a night, and so was I. He was a good baby, rarely cried, and seemingly happy just to sit in the buggy. We took long walks, went shopping, returned home for naps, and I thought, *Wow, this is going to be easy.* Ha, famous last words!

When he was between one and two years old, I noticed the first red flag: his lack of speech. There was nothing, not even a babble. He would point and grunt if he really wanted something, and he would cry from time to time, but even that was limited. He was quiet and still, and seemed always absorbed in whatever he was doing. Interest in one toy could last for hours. I remember thinking how great it was that I could just put Jackie in his rocker, give him his set of plastic keys, and he'd be fine, while my friends would scramble around every five minutes trying to entertain their screaming toddlers. But the delayed speech became more of an issue with me as time went on. At Jackie's two-year pediatrician visit, I brought it up. The doctor did a few quick hearing exercises and that checked out. She explained to me that children develop language at different rates and that he should begin the process soon. So I waited and worked on it with him, singing nursery rhymes, and trying to get him to repeat momma and daddy, but all I got was a repetitive *Da*.

Just when I was beginning to get really nervous about his lack of speech, the big moment came. It was soon after his second birthday. I walked into his bedroom, and he was standing in his crib playing with his stuffed Tigger, his favorite Disney character. He held up Tigger and said, "Tigger lifted his ear fiercely." I stood in complete shock as Tigger was flung, with a giggle, from his hands like a projectile, aimed at my face. Who is this child? Where did he come from? And the talking didn't end there. Over the course of several weeks, I heard: "It's a blustery day outside. My tummy is rumbly," and "Let's go for a walk in the garden."

Jackie went from zero to sixty in the blink of an eye and I thought, *Wow, he's a genius. He's going to be in advanced everything when school starts. Maybe he'll even skip a grade.* I soon realized that though he was talking, it really wasn't communication as most of us experience it. It was all mimicry. I would ask him a question, and he might not answer. Then he would chime in with something that may or may not be a part of the conversation but were all repetitions of various parts of songs or television shows that were stuck in his head. This continued into the school years. As he got older, it became easier to decipher what was mimicry and what were really his own thoughts. We went quickly from Winnie the Pooh to Thomas the Tank Engine to Sponge Bob. In the end, I think that it was just his way of learning language. I could have a complete conversation with him at times and think that they were really his words and thoughts speaking back to me, and then suddenly, I'd get a Sponge Bob answer and realize that he wasn't present at all.

I remedied this by stopping the conversation and asking, "Where's that saying from?" This brought him back to me, he would tell me where he had heard it, and then we could continue on, having a real conversation for a while.

Even today, he fixates on certain sayings and has to repeat them repeatedly. Most recently, his friends told me that the saying of the week was, "On a scale from one to ten, how would you rate your pain?" I have no idea where that came from, and I'm sure I don't need to know.

The second red flag that I noticed early on was that he didn't seem to want to crawl. The day after his first birthday, he went from sitting to just standing up and walking. It was kind of amazing, actually, and I thought, *OK, why bother with crawling when walking gets you there faster.* But the missed step did make me feel a little uncomfortable. There was a nagging question in my mind: *Is this a good thing, or are other issues coming?*

So, I shoved that dark thought deep down and tried to think positively, telling myself that I was just being paranoid. Mostly, the first few years seemed typical. I was bracing myself for the terrible twos, but they never came. He was quiet and seemingly happy and never a problem. No big tantrums, no mood changes, no negativity. We just went on with our schedule: fun trips to the park, bike rides, home for naps. And then around the age of four, everything changed, and that nagging question came back in full force.

It really began with the onset of sensory issues. Jackie became a fussy eater who went from trying anything to accepting only four or five foods. He could no longer tolerate tags in his shirts or belts around his waist. Collared shirts begot tantrums, and baseball caps were out of the question. We could no longer go to loud parades, and the noise of an ambulance going by would send him into freak-out mode. No restaurants, no circus, no candle stores. He would have a difficult time touching anything textural or warm. To this day, most of this still exists. At the time, all of it seemed to come out of nowhere. One day he was happy and content, and the next he was an angry sensory-overloaded child. Life became more difficult. It took a while to figure out what was going on and, once all of the pieces came together, his pediatrician made the diagnosis of sensory integration disorder. She really thought that he would grow out of it, that as he got older he would "grow into" his senses and get used to the world around him. In my gut, I knew more was coming. We began gross motor therapy to help him become more in tune with his body and tried to get him involved in anything tactile to help desensitize him from some of the touch issues that he had. Unfortunately, sensory integration issues at the time were not recognized by insurance companies as a viable diagnosis for treatment. Now I not only had to deal with Jackie's issue, but also the insurance company's reluctance to cover the cost. And so began my battle with them. Writing letters to our insurance company became a monthly ritual. Trying to figure out what codes our therapists should use, so that the therapies would be accepted under our policy and paid for, was a nightmare.

In the end, none of the therapies really seemed to help. All they did was make him angry—so much so that it was sometimes impossible to get to our appointment at all. In time, I just decided that it really wasn't a big deal to cut the tags out of his clothes or bring noise reducing headphones to loud events. The doctor had told me that sensory issues usually iron themselves out, so I waited. For the next year, I avoided the places that would be difficult for Jackie. If we wanted to go out for dinner, I'd make sure there was seating available outside, where the food odors wouldn't be so strong. At the Fourth of July parade, I'd have his earphones ready and an easy escape plan if I saw him stressing out. I became more in sync with Jackie's behaviors and learned to look for signs of his discomfort. I kept telling myself that by kindergarten, it would all be worked out. Just a few more years, and he would be like every other kid in his class. But some of the truth came well before his school days, and it came just as the sensory problems did: out of nowhere like a punch to the gut.

CHAPTER TWO

One December day, when Jackie was five, we waited in line for half an hour for Jackie to see Santa, sit on his lap, and tell him all about the cool dump truck that he wanted for Christmas. Other children ran around, their happy shouts echoed off the mall ceiling, and their sticky candy canes dropped to the carpet. Jackie stood close to me as he covered his ears with his hands and turned his face away from the madness he saw. By the time we reached the woman dressed up in an elf costume and saw the soft lap of Santa, it was too late. He broke out in tears and refused to approach the rosy-cheeked man. It was all too much—the noise, the waiting, and the running around. We left sad and with the worry that Santa would never know what he wanted for a Christmas gift. After a while, I got smart and found a great website to send and receive letters to and from Santa. Thank God for the Internet.

The sensory integration diagnosis was still in place, but there had been little improvement and no adjustment to his behavior showing me that things were calming down. If anything, it was all getting worse. It had become common practice for Jackie to hide during preschool. He was often found alone in the empty block room trying to escape the noise of the classroom. He wouldn't engage with the other children, continued playing alone, and would become upset the moment a friend would try to join in. But, still, it all sort of fit in with the idea of sensory issues. Then one day, when I went to pick up Jackie from preschool, the teacher pulled me aside.

"We had an incident today," she said. My first thought was that he had bitten someone out of frustration. The thing I'd often heard about—the kids that bite. She led me over to a corner, while the other mothers came and went. "Today Jackie went missing." I glanced over to where he was moving a red, plastic car back and forth over a carpeted road. "We couldn't find him for a long time, and then I finally checked the bathroom and there he was." *OK*, I thought. *That's not too bad.* The teacher looked at me seriously then as if she was afraid to tell me the rest of it. She took a deep breath. "He had taken the finger paints from the easel with him and had painted every bit of wall space in the bathroom with his hands."

My first response was, "Did it get cleaned up?" I think I was in shock.

"Yes," she replied. "But I think that this behavior is a little odd." She was right. Jackie hated finger paints—hated anything slimy on his hands. If he had wanted to paint, he could have used the easel. Why decide to paint the bathroom? I have to admit that, at the time, a small part of me saw humor in it, but a bigger part was becoming increasingly nervous.

"Maybe it's a part of his sensory thing," I suggested.

"Maybe."

The pieces were coming together. I knew in that moment that it wouldn't be long before we had something else to deal with and, in a way, I was ready. The diagnosis of sensory integration wasn't getting us anywhere. I wanted answers. I wanted to be able to help him in so many ways: making friends, communicating better, and understanding emotion. It was so frustrating not comprehending all that was going on with him, blaming everything on the sensory issues, even when it didn't really fit. I began to notice new behaviors at home. He would spend hours lining up

cars in a straight row until we had a traffic jam leading from the front door of the house to the back. If
I moved any of them even a fraction of an inch, he
would be upset. If I took one away and replaced it
with a different car, he would notice immediately. It
was also very difficult for him to understand that, at
some point, we would need to put them away. This
led to transitions being very difficult. We'd have to
deconstruct the highway in stages. He would line up
the cars, and then I would say, "OK, on Sunday we
will need to move them to another area that isn't in
the middle of the house." He would find a less con-
spicuous place, maybe under a table, and we would
move them. Then in another few days, we would put
half of the cars away, and then by the end of that
week, we would be able to put them in his room.
This seemed to be the process for everything…grad-
ual steps, letting him make some of the decisions so
that he felt comfortable.

Jackie also began to fixate on numbers. Each day
would begin with a number. If it was six, then we had
to turn the light on and off six times, or he would
have to repeat a certain phrase six times. Some days
I got lucky, and the number was two. Other days, we
ended up with twenty-four. It was hard to be patient.
Today he fixates on one number: nine, but it's a lot
easier. If there's a nine on the clock, we can't leave
a room. If he ends a computer game with his score

including a nine, he can't stop. If a video is nine minutes, then he needs to watch another. No more flipping on lights or repeating phrases any more.

The other thing that I began to notice was that Jackie was becoming easily frustrated and angry. If he wanted to go to the park, and I told him that we didn't have time, he might have a huge tantrum. If he wanted ice cream for dinner, to wear shorts when it was snowing outside, or wanted to stay up until one o'clock in the morning and I said no, he would turn into a screaming, out-of-control two-year-old. It was like the terrible sixes instead of the terrible twos, and Jackie was big for his age. You can imagine how that looked out in public.

The eating issues became worse, and we were concerned that he might stop eating altogether. We took him to a nutritionist who took one look at the few things he was eating: graham crackers, wheat bread, and peanut butter, and told us that we should only give him the foods that we wanted him to eat. Her philosophy was that if he doesn't eat the chicken and rice casserole, he'd just have to go hungry. I put the plate of chicken nuggets and applesauce in front of him night after night. My heart was in my throat as he cried and cried, not touching a thing. In desperation, I took a spoonful of applesauce, waited for him to scream, and forced it into his mouth. I thought that if he just tried it, he would end up liking it, and that one new thing might open up a whole new world of food. What I got was a plate full of vomit as he gagged on the overly sweet spoonful. He lost 10 percent of his body weight in two weeks, and the pediatrician told me to stop.

Kindergarten came and then first grade, and I thought, *Now we'll see a change.* Being around other children all day long, eating in the lunchroom, giving into peer pressure, and finally eating a slice of pizza—all these things would finally help him grow out of the sensory integration nightmare that we were all living in. He made a friend or two and was invited to more than a few birthday parties. Out came the pizza and over to the corner went Jackie, as far away as he could get from the smells. Other children began to notice, asking why he didn't like pizza, and what could he say? I became his voice explaining that the tastes were just too strong for him. The sensory overload went on and on, and I knew that there just had to be more to it. I had never met another mother who was going through any of this, all my friends kept telling me that he would grow out of it, and the doctors didn't really understand it. I was scared and completely stressed out, but I just had to keep working with what I had.

And so, with all of this going on and Jackie still having a difficult time making friends, in the summer before second grade I decided to send him to a new camp. My hope was that in this outside environ-ment, he would be less overwhelmed. I thought that the fun atmosphere would help him feel more com-fortable to maybe try a hotdog or encourage him to make a new friend. Maybe if he saw other children playing games together, he might join in. When I dropped him off on that first day, he was nervous; so was I. But after meeting the counselors, Jackie seemed to relax, and they led him to an art project where a few other children were working. After a few minutes, he forgot that I was still there and seemed content to watch other children glue macaroni to wooden sticks. During the morning, I was hopeful. No phone calls, no panicked counselors calling to tell me to pick up my crying son. Several hours later, as I arrived at the campground to pick him up, I was excited to see whom he had spent his time with, maybe even meet the other mother, set up a play-date. Unfortunately, what I saw was Jackie curled up under a tree crying his eyes out, alone. When he saw me, he ran to me and began telling me stories of bullies, kids hurting him, kids trying to kill him. He was in complete fear, shaking, saying he would never come back to this camp. My heart sank, and I found myself in complete saber-toothed tiger mode, ready to hunt down the bullies and confront their parents, ready to attack the counselors and demand an expla-nation as to why these bullies weren't ejected from the camp. It was then that the head counselor approached me and pulled me aside.

"What's going on?" I asked, trying to keep my voice calm and failing miserably. He was a nice looking young man, just out of college, and I could see from the look on his face that there was more to the story. I wanted answers.

"Jackie had a rough day," he said.

"He told me that the kids were being mean to him," I retorted, and he quickly told me the story. They had decided to play dodgeball. They divided into teams and passed out the rubber balls. Jackie had never played dodgeball. When the opposite team began throwing the balls, he ran away. This continued until the counselor could see that he was visibly upset, and so he took him out of the game to play with another boy who didn't like the game. When that boy tried to toss a ball to Jackie, he continued to run away upset. The counselor looked at me uncomfortably as I ran the story through my mind. I could understand not liking dodgeball, but being in complete fear, thinking that there were kids trying to kill you. That just seemed weird.

The counselor continued, "I don't want to assume anything, but I work with autistic children during the school year, and Jackie seems to have many of the same traits as my students." I was dumbfounded, but grateful, too. In hindsight, it made sense. Jackie had misread the other children's intentions in the dodgeball game. He couldn't understand why they were throwing balls at him, trying to hurt him. The next day, I called my doctor and made the appointment for an evaluation.

CHAPTER THREE

The diagnostic process for Autism Spectrum Disorder was an all-day process. It involved a neurologist, a pediatrician, and a therapist all meeting with Jackie, asking him questions, and engaging him in activities. Thirty minutes into the evaluation, as I sat in the adjacent room watching through a two-way mirror, the neurologist stepped in to chat.

"Honestly, I can't believe that Jackie hasn't been diagnosed before this."

"Really?" I replied in shock. "Well, we've always just thought he had sensory issues." She looked long at me then, sizing me up, trying to determine how much I could handle. She must have seen something strong in my face, even though in that moment I felt two inches tall.

"I have to be honest," she said. "I knew he was on the spectrum after about ten minutes of talking to him." My eyes flicked to the mirror where Jackie's face appeared. He was fixated with his face, unable to detach himself from his reflection.

"See," the doctor said with a smile. "He can't stop looking at himself. He is an island, in his own head, and he is most comfortable when the world around him is calm." As she continued to explain all the behaviors that many ASD kids have: the social problems, the restricted interests, the repetitive behaviors, and communication impairment, the light went on in my head. Jackie's obsession with cars, his inability to make friends, the latent speech and his fear of numbers, it all fit. She also told me that many times ASD begins with sensory issues but that sensory issues don't always lead to ASD. The diagnosis of ASD is, many times, difficult to arrive at early on. This is because it really has such a big social piece. Looking back, I can see the red flags that, at the time, I thought were just the sensory issues. I know now that when Jackie painted that bathroom in preschool, it was one of his first moments of self-regulating. Internally, he was anxious, or his internal system overloaded and the repetition of painting on the walls was probably soothing.

The diagnosis of Autism Spectrum Disorder came as a shock, but I was also relieved. Now I had answers, now I could do my research, and now I could help him. But I also felt sad for Jackie. It was the beginning of the list of all of the childhood events that he would miss, the things that I had such fond memories of as a child. The circus, visits to see Santa and the Easter bunny, Twinkies and McDonald's, the freedom of living alone at college—would he even be able to experience that? Would he ever have close friends? Would he ever be able, socially, to hold down a job? What would all of this mean for his future? I decided, in that moment, that I would do whatever it took to help make his life the best that it could be. I would have to parent differently. I would have to try not to react to his behavior but instead try to understand it from a different vantage point. I knew it wouldn't be easy, but I certainly didn't realize the difficulties I would face.

After the diagnosis of ASD, we entered into the world of the Individual Education Plan (IEP), a plan to help Jackie academically as well as emotionally within the school system. This included speech therapy and social therapy during the school day. As I began my education about autism and how Jackie's mind worked, the sensory issues moved lower on the crisis list. In the early years of his diagnosis, the difference between his behavior and his peers' was not as noticeable. This was good and bad.

Jackie began to develop a few friendships based on a similar interest in cars, but they didn't always last. Unfortunately, several of Jackie's teachers didn't understand ASD. At one point, a teacher told me that all her students had issues to deal with and that all her students had special needs. She went on to add that many of her students had a difficult time making friends and that many were very immature. Jackie was really no different. I watched her face fall as I explained that most typical kids with these issues don't come home, break things in their rooms, and talk about killing themselves over friends' not sitting with them at lunch. Most moms aren't banging their heads against the wall trying to get their children to understand that a friend can spend time with someone else and still be their friends, a concept that a black and white thinker can't get.

During much of elementary school, Jackie had one good friend, Alan. He was a nice boy who liked cars and seemed quiet and calm. They always went to lunch together and sat next to each other during class time when they could. We invited him to movies and on trips for ice cream, and for the first time, Jackie seemed to grow emotionally. Of course, with autism, Jackie fixated on one person at a time so Alan was it, but through Alan, Jackie was learning the kind of communication skills and social skills that you just can't get through therapy. It was a great relationship—until it all went terribly wrong.

I got the e-mail from his teacher on a Friday. Jackie had gone up to a girl on the playground and called her a bad name, the worst name you can call a girl. Use your imagination. The girl had been very upset, and the teacher wanted me to come in after school to talk about it. I walked into her classroom and saw Jackie sitting in the book corner, his head buried in a book. He looked bad: blotchy cheeks from crying and eyes full of fear that I might be upset. The teacher welcomed me and asked Jackie to come and join us. He slunk over to his chair.

"Today on the playground Jackie called one of his classmates a bad name. As I have already explained to Jackie, we don't tolerate that kind of behavior in our classroom." Jackie scrunched down in his chair, and I saw his eyes begin to well up. I knew there had to be more to the story. I couldn't imagine where Jackie would have even heard the word in question. We don't swear in our house, and at that point, Jackie wasn't allowed to go on playdates without me. So I turned to him and asked him to tell me what happened.

"Alan told me to say it," he replied. "He said that it would make her laugh." The first thought that came into my mind was, *if Alan jumped off a mountain would you follow him?* But I didn't say that. I knew that his excuse sounded like what any kid would say if he got busted. The first rule of deviant children: if you're caught, blame it on someone else. However, I knew that Jackie was incapable of lying. He was incapable of rationally sitting down and thinking out an excuse. He's a tell-it-like-it-is kind of guy—again, a black and white thinker. The teacher interrupted my thoughts.

"I asked Alan if he had told Jackie to say the bad word, and he said no. Since there was no proof other than Jackie actually saying the word, I had to give Jackie a consequence today." That consequence took the form of Jackie being made to sit at a desk and watch as his classmates enjoyed a party and game time without him. I found out later that he sat with his head down on his desk sobbing uncontrollably. I was dumbfounded. Though the consequence was bad, Jackie was tortured by the idea that a friend could not only tell him to say a bad word but then also not come forward and tell the truth. The social game now became even more confusing for him.

The first thing I did was turn to my son and tell him that I believed him, that I knew that he would have never done this on his own. I also talked to him about the importance of questioning things that his friends might tell him to do, to ask a teacher first. The second thing I did was talk to the teacher about how unfair the consequence seemed both to Jackie and to me. To put a child through that type of emotional distress bordered on abuse, and that it might have been more helpful to sit the three children down to talk about it with the social worker.

The third thing that I did was to call a meeting with Jackie's social work staff to adjust his IEP. I called for an end to negative reinforcement as a way to deal with situations like this. I told them that because of this one consequence, Jackie was now confused and angry and had learned nothing other than not to trust your friends. I also asked that if Jackie were in a similar situation where he became the target of bullying, not to include negative reinforcement as a solution, even to the bully. I asked them to first try to figure out why the behavior was happening and then fix it.

The last thing that I did was to make a very big decision. I decided to talk openly to Jackie and those around me about his autism. After the playground incident, I began to think about how easy it would be for Jackie to fall into that same kind of situation again. I also felt bad for the girl in Jackie's class. I knew that it must have been very hurtful to be called a name, and I suspected that her idea of Jackie had probably changed because of it. I now had a little boy who didn't understand what was wrong with him. He would sit in his bed and ask me repeatedly, "Why did this happen? Why is it so hard for me to have a friend? Why don't people understand me? Why don't I understand them?" It was tough. I wanted to explain to him all that was going on in his brain, about the autism, but the doctors had cautioned me about telling him too soon. They worried that he wouldn't understand. So I kept saying, "It's your issue, Jackie. It's something that you just can't control." I began to feel like I was hiding this dirty little secret: autism. And by hiding it, I was turning it into a very negative thing. I didn't want that for him. I didn't want him ever to think that there was anything wrong with him. I also wanted his friends to have a word that explained his behaviors. Autism will always be a *part* of who he is but not *all* of who he is, so I made the decision when he was in third grade to "tell it like it is."

"The reason why you don't always understand your friends and they don't understand you is because you have autism."

"Oh."

And that was it. After that day he had a word that answered his questions, we talked about it all the time. We would break down situations that happened during the day and figure out what part of it was because of the autism and what part of it was just being a kid. We kept a journal so that if the same situations came up again, we could look back and see what our thoughts had been before. It helped me compartmentalize his behavior so that I could always tell what needed to be worked on and then explain this to his teachers. When your ASD child is young, immature, and seems to blend right in with his peers, it can be difficult to explain what ASD looks like. For us, those differences were more apparent at home, where he felt safe to decompress after school. And though many of the situations that affected Jackie seemed like normal everyday kid issues, the way that Jackie saw them and dealt with them were anything but average. Simple issues such as how to maintain friendships, understanding emotion, and analyzing the reactions of others were not always concrete ideas to him. Through his development and interactions with others, he hadn't learned those lessons. Teaching them now was like trying to teach him a foreign language. Not easy.

When I picked Jackie up from school, he immediately began to cry. My heart sank. What had happened now? He said that he had been out in the school field playing soccer with a few friends. He and his new best friend, Hank (Alan had been removed from the equation) were on one team, and two other boys were on the other. They were goofing around a lot, not taking the game too seriously at first, but then the game switched, and both sides were really trying to win. Hank got close to the goal and pulled his leg back ready to smack the ball into the net when he was caught off balance and ended up kicking the ball in the wrong direction, missing the goal by a mile. Jackie began to laugh loudly, not noticing the hurt look on Hank's face, unable to distinguish a hurt look from a happy or indifferent expression. Hank turned to Jackie and said, "You're a jerk, and you're not my friend anymore."

He was so worried that he had lost his only friend in the world, yet again, and didn't understand why. That was a tough one for me. I wanted to call Hank's mom and explain that Jackie can't always tell when someone's upset, and that he doesn't always know when a game goes from goofing around to serious. If Hank had just told Jackie that he was upset because of the laughing, Jackie would have felt bad and said he was sorry. But I could see how Hank had every right to be upset, too, how maybe I was asking too much of a fourth grader. Maybe it was too much to think that Hank might understand things from Jackie's point of view. I did contact his mother, and I explained the ASD and how it had contributed to the misunderstanding. She was so nice about it, but I got the same words that I usually got from another parent with a typical child: *all kids have disagreements, and then they're friends the next day. Jackie's just like everyone else his age.* That's always disappointing to hear. What those words say to me is *I don't care about the ASD, I don't want to learn about it, and you're overreacting.* It's not that I wish his ASD to be more severe or that I want him to stand out as different, but because he can blend in on the surface, other parents sometimes make me feel as if I'm exaggerating my frustrations. I know they probably mean well, but those comments make it worse.

The backlash of it all was horrible. I wish I could have had Hank's mom over to witness that. Jackie cried for twelve hours straight until he finally fell asleep. He was afraid to go back to school even after hours of conversation about how friends have disagreements all the time and that I was sure that Hank would come around. I encouraged him to apologize, but he was afraid of that, too. This was the first time that I heard Jackie talk about how he shouldn't be alive anymore, words that I would hear often as he got older. Of course, it all worked out in the end. Hank got over his anger, and Jackie continued to hang out with him until Hank was transferred to another school. But I knew that things had to change. I knew that somehow I needed to let people know that ASD is real. No one else saw the anger that seemed to be over a substitute teacher showing up in class. No one else saw the continuous self-loathing over lost friendships that really weren't lost at all. No one else saw the freak-outs over a bowl of watermelon that was perceived as blood. I wanted my community, at least, to know that our kids are different, that it's OK, and that it would be great if they could meet us halfway and try to understand some of it. I felt that people should know about these things. I felt that people should know about Jackie— the good, bad, and the ugly. With all of this in mind and as Jackie's journal entries grew, I asked him how he would feel about turning his journal into a published book. He was thrilled, not only to be a published author but also to share his story with other kids who might think like him. I felt that if nothing else came from it, the book would be a great way to begin a conversation about autism. And so, *Jackie's Journal* was born.

CHAPTER FOUR

When I was in college, I worked with Susan, an adult with Down syndrome. I would take her to the pool, shopping, or on walks. It was a challenging job. One day, her mother asked if I would take Susan down to the DMV to get an ID made. She would never be able to drive, but it made sense for her to have some sort of official identification, so I agreed. As I stood with Susan at the counter trying to explain what we needed, the man looked at me with confusion. He was older with that kind of comb-over hair, clearly trying to hide his bald spot. He called his partner over, and I explained once again that what we needed was an identification card and that

I had a birth certificate and proof of address with me. They glanced over the information and asked, "Is this for you or for her?" The balding man jabbed a stubby finger at Susan. I think that they were confused that I was doing all of the talking.

Susan let out a laugh and exclaimed, "It's for you! It's for you! You can be Susan," in the sing-song voice of a four-year old.

I saw the recognition of Down syndrome all over their faces as the balding man leaned into his partner and whispered, "Oh, she's a retard." Susan got her ID, but that moment stayed with me. In that moment, I knew that I could never handle having a special needs kid. It was too much work. It was embarrassing, frustrating, and sad. I thought of how Susan's parents would have to take care of her for the rest of their lives, and how Susan would never lead anything close to a normal life. I thought about my options should I discover that a child I might be carrying would be like Susan one day. What would I do?

Of course, years later I had Jackie. At the time of my pregnancy, I had no way of knowing that he would be a special needs child; I just knew that I would love him no matter what. It simply wouldn't have mattered what those special needs turned out to be. He was still my boy. That's the way it is when you have children. When they're yours, the love you feel transcends all of the problems that you might face—at least it did for me. So as difficult as it's been dealing with all of the problems that come with growing up and puberty and ASD, we have always chosen to celebrate the things that make up Jackie. We have chosen to focus on the positive as much as we can and not to put too much emphasis on the negative. His photographic memory for all things that interest him, his knowledge of cars, his medals for Science Olympiad, all of the chess trophies, and his recent induction into the National Junior Honor Society, are all causes for celebration. I have always tried to guide him to those things that I thought he could excel at, hoping to increase the positive and balance the scale in that direction. It hasn't always worked.

Shortly after the release of Jackie's book, I was speaking at a Barnes & Noble one rainy afternoon to a group of educators and parents. The presentation was mainly about our struggles but also about the celebrations. Sometimes we get so caught up in the struggle that we forget all the good in our kids. I wanted the parents and teachers to understand the importance of the positive in special needs children's lives. After the talk was over, a man, the father of an older ASD child, approached me. He looked long at me and said, "I gave your son's book to my son to read, and it made him very upset." I felt horrible, but I couldn't understand how this could happen.

"I'm so sorry," I replied.

"He was jealous because he saw all the things that Jackie could do and knew that he wasn't like him."

"Oh, no."

"I just don't see how you can celebrate something like autism, and I really think that you should stick with talking about higher-functioning autism. My son has never been high functioning, and he doesn't have a great memory, or the ability to write a book, or even the smarts to be in a typical classroom. His life has been hard." I thought about his words. I worried that maybe I shouldn't be the voice for kids like his son. Maybe I needed to put our situation in the Asperger's box and focus on that. But I knew deep down that my life—that Jackie's life—wasn't about Asperger's or even ASD. It was about helping all kids feel worthy and helping them realize that it's OK to be different.

"Tell me about your son," I said.

"Well, he's twenty-one, and he lives with his grandparents. He has a difficult time holding down a job, but he occasionally bags groceries for the local store. He wants to fit in and gets very upset because he never does." I nod knowingly. Jackie never feels like he fits in.

"What does he like to do during his time off? Does he have any interests?"

"No, not really," replied the man. "He spends most of his time helping out his grandparents around the house. He'll help move heavy boxes for them or do the laundry. He likes to garden with them and, for some reason, he likes to clean the floors." That information was enough for me to see the real problem here.

"You know, not all of us have gifts that are smacking us in the face like Jackie's knowledge of all things car related. Sometimes we have to look deeper to find the celebration. If your son is sad because he can't memorize facts, tell him I said that Jackie would *never* clean the floors or do the laundry for me. And I don't know any twenty-one-year-old men who would take such good care of their grandparents. That's his gift; he's a caretaker, and that's a pretty important gift. That's worthy of a celebration." The man just looked at me, his mouth open in amazement. And then, slowly, he began to smile.

"Look," I continued. "I'm not trying to speak about things that I don't understand. I'm just trying to get the message out that we all have gifts to share with the world—all of us. It's up to us as parents and as educators to dig those gifts out and to make sure that our children know about them. Then we just need to help the world accept them." It was a breakthrough moment for this man, I think. Like many of us, he had gotten caught up in the day-to-day drama, and it had pulled him down. I was hoping that, now, his celebration would begin.

Believe me when I say that not every day is a celebration around my house. The frustration of constantly trying to get Jackie to understand the simplest things has been exhausting: trying to explain to him that if he doesn't turn off his iPad within the next five minutes, there's a good chance that he'll be late for school. Giving him several more warnings as the minutes tick away, only to be blamed and yelled at by him because we didn't make it before the first bell. There's a constant lack of taking responsibility, and when things don't go the way he wants them to, it's not because he didn't listen, it's because I never told him in the first place. The things that I go through now make my past life with Susan seem laughably simple. And constantly, my friends ask me how I do it. The answer is that I just do.

My sister, Ellen, was born with a congenital birth defect in her heart. She was in the hospital a lot as a child, first having surgeries to repair the hole, and then more surgeries for valve replacement. My dad was working full time while going on to further his education. My mom was working full time to help with the financial burden of it all. There were three of us kids: my brother, Mike, the oldest, Ellen next, and then me. I asked my mom how she managed, how she held down that secretarial job during the day and then drove an hour to the hospital to be with Ellen only to have to race home again to make dinner and be with the rest of us. She seemed like superwoman to me, someone who could do anything. She told me that it wasn't easy, but you do what you have to do; you don't think about it; you just do it. Those words come back to me in my dark days, and I know that we'll get through the difficult times because what choice do we have? My sister's in great health now, since the valve was replaced with the ticking synthetic mechanical one. My parents are retired. Some days, I can't wait for the day when I can just be alone, when I can get rid of all the stress. But I know that once that day comes, the day that I send him off to college, I'll be wishing that Jackie were back with me—drama and all. So until that day, I try to remember that man at my book signing and his son. I continue to try to find the celebration in my life and in Jackie's. And mostly, I try not to think too far ahead or worry about what the future will bring. Either way, we'll have to get through it. What choice do we have?

CHAPTER FIVE

The summer before fifth grade, I asked Jackie how he would feel about sharing *Jackie's Journal* with his classmates. This would mean talking openly about ASD and letting everyone know that this was something that he dealt with. He was all for it, partially because he liked the idea of potentially being famous, but also because he wanted to be understood and wanted others like him to know that they weren't alone. Jackie stood in front of his classmates, holding his book, answering question after question about how his mind worked. There were a lot of *aha* moments and comments like, *Oh, that's why sometimes Jackie seems to have too much energy,* or *Oh, that's why*

Jackie has a hard time in the cafeteria, or *I was wondering why he didn't know I was joking and got upset.* My hope was that once his peers knew and understood ASD a little better, they would become more understanding of kids like Jackie. I wondered if now, instead of jumping to assumptions about his behavior, they might stop and think about it and react differently. Some did, and some didn't, but it was a start.

That was the beginning of many lessons I had to share. It was the opening of the conversation regarding ASD, and even though the children seemed to want to know more, some educators just wanted to go on with business as usual. It's hard to break free from already-formed assumptions. I found that a few of Jackie's teachers didn't even want to try to understand some of his behaviors. It was easier to just blend him in and act as if the IEP didn't exist. But I have always been a believer that the best way to parent or teach an ASD kid is also the best way to parent or teach any kid. Kindness, understanding, positive reinforcement, and emotional security are the factors that I try to keep in mind. I'm a believer in mutual respect, regardless of age.

I knew that my battles were just beginning and that someday my battles would become Jackie's. It seemed as if I shuffled phone calls and e-mails back and forth every day with a teacher or the school social worker. There were constant problems in the beginning, with teachers or social workers always wanting to figure out how to get Jackie to fit in. The diagnosis was still so new to me, and I tried to go along with the program, trying to get Jackie to understand all of the social issues that seemed to anger him. He just didn't understand his peers or about personal space, he couldn't tolerate any unexpected change that might occur, and homework organization was difficult. By the end of fifth grade, the teachers were beginning to encourage independence in their students, giving them tasks without reminders and special jobs within the classroom. It was about this time that everything changed for me. It was the first time that I realized that, really, Jackie's well-being was up to me.

I got a phone call from Jackie's teacher one Friday afternoon. Jackie had had a hard day, and she wondered if she might meet with me after school. I was beginning to wonder if it might be a good idea just to set up a standing weekly meeting. I felt like I was there almost as much as the students were. I walked into the classroom and saw Jackie sitting at a long table, looking very afraid. I smiled reassuringly, but he only glanced to the teacher, clearly thinking he was in deep trouble.

"So, what's going on?" I asked, trying to keep it lighthearted. Whatever happened, I knew that we would work it out. I couldn't understand Jackie's fear.

"Well, Jackie has had an upsetting day," the teacher replied, glancing toward him. He looked down. I sat in the empty chair between them and put my arm around Jackie.

"I'm sorry to hear that," I said.

Without hesitation, the teacher continued. "I had to give Jackie a consequence today." I noticed immediately that she conveniently left out the word *negative* before the word *consequence*. She paused, giving Jackie a knowing glance. He didn't see it. He just kept looking at his hands in his lap. "Yesterday, I gave the class a form to take home. They were supposed to have a parent sign it and then bring it back today. Jackie seems to have forgotten to get a signature and, because of that, he will have to miss an hour of the end-of-year party." My mind began the process of flipping back through the list of things we did the night before. Therapy after school, a little homework…oh, yeah, I remembered him telling me about the form, and then it hit me. Jackie had asked me to sign the form five times while doing homework. I kept forgetting, and every time he asked, I would tell him that it was next on my list. He was obsessing over the signature, anxious about it, worried and fixated, so typically ASD. Finally, right before bed, he asked me one more time so, out of irritation, I did something that I try never to do—I lied.

"Yes, Jackie, I already did it. Don't worry." I had meant to go right downstairs and sign the form, but unfortunately, the phone rang so I got distracted and, yes, I forgot. I felt horrible, and I explained all of this to his teacher. I also told her that Jackie had been obsessing over it and that the push for independence was really just creating worry and anxiety for him. The truth was that he just might not have been ready. I was shocked when she informed me that she stood by her decision and that Jackie could have checked his folder that morning to make sure that the signature was there. I couldn't control the tenor of my voice. I was verging on livid.

"So, you think that my son should have doubted me when I told him that I signed the form?" Silence. "And I'd like to know what happened to the new IEP notes that specifically state that negative reinforcement is not an option for him." Silence. "I would think that your time would be better spent trying to figure out why a child might have trouble getting organized instead of punishing him when he's not." Jackie sank lower and lower in his chair. I noticed a slight grin, but the fear was still in his eyes. He was probably afraid that I was going to hit his teacher. I spotted his backpack perched next to him and I unzipped it, pulling out his folder. The form is there, right in front, jeering at me. I grabbed the pen in front of me on the table, signed the form, and slid it over to the teacher.

"Here it is, signed and handed in today." Silence again. "Are you ready, Jackie?" I asked as I stood to leave. I knew there would be another conversation to come, one involving the social work staff and possibly the principal, but I had gained something from this experience. I realized that I had a real fighter in me. I realized that teachers might not always know best. And I realized that, though we had a really good IEP, it was up to me to make sure that it was enforced.

When the big realization came to me—the idea that maybe the school system doesn't always know what's best for my son—I began to think about autism differently. Autism is a neurological issue—a brain issue—and the brain can sometimes be rewired. It is possible to retrain the brain to some level. I grew up with dyslexia, also a neurological issue. In school, I was unable to read. Back then, in the seventies, no one understood dyslexia, and I slipped through the cracks. As I entered college, I realized that I was an auditory learner and so I never missed a class and did well. Homemade flash cards became my best friend. The repetitive learning worked wonders for me, and by the end of college, there were shopping bags full of used cards piled high in my closet. As an adult, I began the process of retraining my brain. I did this by listening to audiobooks while reading them and then reading them again and again. Today, I know that this is a process used in schools to help dyslexic children. I still have dyslexia. I can read better, but there are still times when the letters are jumping off the page, or I can't verbally get the thoughts out of my head. Like me, Jackie can also do some things to retrain his brain to a certain degree. He can learn to stop and filter his thoughts before he speaks, he can learn to control his anger, and he can learn to keep it together during the school day. But he still has autism. He will always have autism and will have to learn how to deal with it. He may never be able to eat at restaurants because of the odor. He may never be able to work in customer service jobs or sales or be able to wear a suit and tie all day, every day. But we all have our limitations and knowing them makes our decisions easier sometimes.

When Jackie was in fifth grade, he decided that he would try taking the bus to school. I thought that this would be a great way for him to build some independence, and it worked for a while. It was a short bus ride, maybe ten blocks, but as with most school busses, it was also a loud ride. One morning when it was time to go to the corner to meet the bus, he became anxious. He had that fear look on his face, the same one he had on the first day of summer camp.

He saw the bus coming and glanced from me to the bus and back and forth until the yellow doors were open and the driver was waving him on. He couldn't get on. His feet wouldn't move, and I realized that something must have happened on that bus, something that he was too afraid to tell me. After retreating to the house, it all came out. The day before, a boy had turned around in his seat and leaned over to punch Jackie in the face. He was so confused by the action and so stunned that he didn't know what to do. I was shocked as well. I'd seen rough video footage on the news, the videos of rowdy middle-school children hitting one another while the bus driver just kept going. I never thought for a moment that that kind of thing could happen on an elementary school bus. I was devastated and felt so angry and guilty. The protocol for this type of thing is to call the school, so that's what I did. The other boy was brought into the principal's office, and it turned out to be a boy that we knew. He said that Jackie kept kicking the back of his seat. It really bothered him so he had asked Jackie to stop, but he wouldn't so he turned around and hit him. It was wrong, of course, and the boy felt bad.

I decided to take a ride on the bus to try to figure out the dynamics of what had happened. I let Jackie get on first and then I quickly ran to another stop a few blocks down. The moment I stepped onto the bus the atmosphere punched me in the face. The noise, the constant seat changing, and the odor of stale lunch and spilled milk hit me hard. I quickly sat down and glanced back to Jackie. He was sitting with a friend, but he wasn't engaging. His friend was talking to the boy across the aisle, looking out the window, laughing at a water bottle as it went zooming by on the black-treaded floor. Jackie sat agitated, his eyes wandering from the window to the front of the bus and then to the back. His leg was swinging a mile a minute, hitting the seat in front of him. He looked like he wanted to run, or scream, or even jump out of the window, and it became clear that the leg swinging was his way of releasing the anxious energy, a way to keep him sane. So with all of this, why did he want to ride the bus in the first place? It turned out that his best friend at the time rode the bus and that Jackie had just wanted to make sure that when he got to school, his friend would be by his side. He was nervous about arriving at school alone.

The sensory overload created a repetitive pattern that Jackie used to release some of his anxiety, but in turn, this behavior had appeared to another boy to be an intentional act of aggression. This made me nervous. Would Jackie's behaviors unwittingly lead him to violent situations in the future? As he got older, would his peers come to understand him and his anxiety and accept him? *Out in the real world* soon became a group of words that hovered in my mind as time went by and is still there today. How will Jackie get along out in the real world with real people who really don't care about the *why* of his behavior? At all of the elementary school teacher conferences, Jackie's teachers would tell me how great he was doing, how he's fitting in and handling all the struggles so well. Little did they know that every day after school is crazy land at my house. He learned early on to keep it together at school. He had accommodations in his IEP for situations that were stressful. He could take a sensory break whenever he needed one. He could see the social worker if he felt angry or out of control. If the lunchroom was overwhelming, he could eat in the classroom. All of these plans were great except for the fact that a nine, ten, or eleven-year-old boy really isn't brave enough to contact a social worker on his own, or isn't in tune enough to sense when he might need a sensory break. So instead of resolving issues at school when they happened, he brought the baggage home where he felt comfortable enough to unload. There was also this idea within the school system that IEPs are for the sole purpose of solving educational needs only. Emotional needs are considered your own problem. Accommodations are geared toward helping children academically; if Jackie needed a sensory break, it was to help him focus better on his work, not necessarily to help alleviate anger. In my mind, the academic success of a child is directly related to his or her emotional well-being, and that's how I drove the IEP meetings. At first, there was some resistance, but in the last five years, there has been a switch in educators' thought processes. Now, I think we're all on board with that idea.

CHAPTER SIX

The issues that Jackie deals with are not mutually exclusive, but rather, form a cycle that feeds off itself. Sensory overload can lead to anger or anxiety. Black and white thinking can lead to missed social cues that then, in turn, lead to anger, anxiety, or depression. The emotions associated with all this are reactive and with very little filter use. This means that your job, as a parent, is to be nonreactive. Not always so easy. There have been times that I have screamed at the top of my lungs in a rant of anger and confusion at a behavior that I can't understand. I have forgotten the ASD and my own filter in stressful situations. I have felt that there have been situations where screaming is the only way to get through to him. I have been wrong and apologetic in these moments and have validated it, in my own mind, by thinking that perhaps I'm teaching Jackie that even adults make mistakes. Maybe that lesson is real. The key to understanding is to see the cycle and break it in a nonreactive way.

Jackie met his best friend, Alexander, in the middle of fifth grade, a time when he felt friendless. Alexander had moved midyear from Roger's Park in Chicago, and so he was also friendless, starting over. He comes from a Romanian background and is a first-generation American. They clicked immediately. Alexander is techy and smart—really smart—and loves cars and so met the criteria of what Jackie needed in a friend. I think Alexander was attracted to the wealth of information that Jackie could rattle off and his strange sense of humor. Either way, they hit it off and are still best friends to this day. They talk about someday attending the same university and about how fun it will be to share a house. However, Alexander pays a price for his friendship with Jackie, and the fee is that he is often in the middle of many of Jackie's conflicts.

If Alexander decided to sit with someone else at lunch, this is how Jackie processed the situation:

Confusion. Why would my friend want to sit with someone else?

What does that other dude have that I don't? Who will I sit with now? I don't know what to do.

Frustration. I have no one to sit with. I don't want to eat lunch. I have no friends.

Depression. If Alexander is not sitting with me, then he must not be my friend anymore. No one likes me. I'm alone. I shouldn't be alive.

Anger. I hate that other guy. I wish he would die so that I can have my friend back. Maybe he will die.

This cycle can continue to play repeatedly in his mind. This has happened more than once, and by the time that Jackie got home from this sort of day, he was sure that he had no friends and that he was a terrible person. He was still very angry with the other boy who took Alexander away. Even though we broke the cycle by revisiting the incident many times, and even though the next day he was back with his bestie, the anger lasted a full year. How could his best friend have another friend? I tried to get all three boys together, but the dynamic didn't work. The other boy didn't get along with Jackie, and I think he was also jealous of the relationship between Jackie and Alexander. There was resentment on both sides as, of course, Alexander was stuck in the middle. Many months after the incident, I received a homemade Mother's Day card that went something like this:

> Roses are blue, violets are red
> I would be happy, if that other kid was dead.
> I love you Mom.
> Happy Mother's Day!

OK. It took *two years* for Jackie finally to form a decent relationship with this other boy, and then there was always someone else to be put into the villain role. Alexander has remained constant as Jackie's best friend. He puts up with a lot but I'm sure gains a lot, too.

It seems as though it's always the little things that trigger the cycle, things that are seemingly meaningless, or things that should be easy to get over. I'm sure everyone has felt alone or worried that no one really likes them. That's kind of what middle school is all about, finding your group and gaining self-esteem. But Jackie can't understand social issues like typical kids can. He can't go into his mind, rationalize the situation, and find conclusions that work. A typical kid might be upset if his friend sits with someone else at lunch, but in his head, he can find a way to deal with it. We all go through a process when facing difficult situations. We might have a first reaction of sadness or frustration, but we can usually talk ourselves through it in a matter of minutes. We can usually rationalize others' choices and behaviors in a way that doesn't necessarily have anything to do with us. We can see things from both sides, and usually, we can come to terms with minor disappointments quickly. A year is a long time to hold onto anger. It's a long time to keep revisiting the situation and to continually blame the other kid for Alexander's choice. This was a rarity, and as Jackie got older, we didn't have too many more year-long issues. Just a few.

Other times, the cycle can be broken quickly, and over the years, I have developed a cycle-breaking process that works for us. It involves validation, redirection, and revisiting a situation to talk about what went wrong. The main frustration for many kids with ASD—and maybe even for all kids—is feeling misunderstood. I try to attack parenting from a belief system that children deserve a voice and that there should be no age restriction on respect. Teaching respect involves showing respect, just as showing violence teaches violence in most cases. So this is what I went with.

I waited for Jackie outside the school on a warm spring day. It was fifth grade, and we were beginning to think about the transition into middle school, which was causing a lot of stress. When he exited the school and came walking down the path, he was crying. My first reaction was, *What now?* I wasn't always on the same page as his fifth-grade teacher. She wanted to believe that he could be forced to fit in if she just dealt with him like everyone else.

"What happened?" I asked, as I took his book bag. He couldn't keep his anger in once he saw me. It was time to unload.

He looked me straight in the eyes and said, "You're not going to believe what my teacher is making me do!" I held my breath, anticipating the worst.

"What?" He stomped his foot and let out a tiger-worthy snarl.

"She making me read a book!"

Whoa! How do you react to that statement?

"Just you?" I asked, knowing that I wasn't getting the complete story.

"No. The whole class!" He stomped again. "It's not fair!" Infamous words…it's not fair.

In my head, I thought, *this whole conversation is crazy*. How could he be crying and so angry over a class assignment? I wanted to tell him to get over it, to stop making such a big deal about a book assignment, but I knew that I couldn't. So I replied, "Hmmm, that sounds bad." He sniffed, and he was able to walk to the car.

"It's bad, and I'm not going to do it!" It was time to validate.

"Yep, it's bad. If it were me, I'd be really upset, too." He glanced at me out of the corner of his eye, trying to figure out if I'd meant it, and I did.

"You know that I have dyslexia. When I was in fifth grade, I couldn't read. Every time there was a book assignment, I would get very upset. It was horrible because most of the teachers thought that I was just lazy."

"Yeah, that's not fair," he replied, softly now. The fire was burning down to ashes at that point, but a spark was still there, ready to ignite again. I could see that he was trying to get himself together. I knew that we couldn't talk about it anymore without refueling the fire, so I redirected to a happy place.

"I have an idea. Let's go get ice cream and play a game of chess." He loved that idea since he was sure to demolish me on the chessboard. Nothing makes him happier than *not* losing. So that's what we did, and for an hour, he forgot about the book and got his body regulated again. The revisit piece is the hardest part. I might be able to revisit the issue in a few hours, or it might take a day or two. When we got home, I sat Jackie down and asked him to tell me all about the book assignment. I thought there might be a way to figure it all out. It turned out that his anger was over the fact that his teacher was letting everyone else pick out his or her own book, while he was forced to read what she would pick out for him. I told him that if this were true, then I agreed that it wasn't fair. He was adamant that he would not do the assignment. I e-mailed the teacher and asked her what her thoughts were. In the end, the whole thing had been a misunderstanding. She had intended to take Jackie to the library to pick out his own book. Since Jackie only liked to read nonfiction and mostly nonfiction about cars, she would help him find a fiction novel that might interest him.

"So, I just e-mailed your teacher," I said, as I entered Jackie's room.

"I hope you told her that I'm not doing the assignment!" he spat.

"What she told me was that she would never make you read a book that she had picked out. She was planning to take you to the library tomorrow and help you find a fiction book about cars." He looked long at me, processing the new information. "You misunderstood what she said, or maybe she didn't explain it right, but either way, you will pick the book out."

"Oh, OK. That's fine then."

This approach is great, but it takes a long time to parent an ASD child. The book thing was an easy solve. It can be grueling getting to the truth, finding out the *why* of the behavior. It can be difficult not to react immediately. ASD kids have the same issues—such as making friends and dealing with the stresses of school—as typical kids have, but the path to understanding is long and drawn out. Situations that go wrong, more than not, can't be easily explained to an ASD kid. *Because I said so*, is not a phrase to be used out of frustration, because they need to know why. They cannot resolve conflict without the *why*. As parents, we can't get to the heart of the problem without knowing the *why*. I have discovered that, most of the time, what initially seems to be the reason for a behavior is not the reality of the situation. I think many of his teachers made assumptions too early about certain behaviors. But, really, I think that's true for all kids in general. There is always a deeper reason for behavior, good or bad. It's really my job, as Jackie's mom, to take the time to figure out that deeper reason, regardless of how tired I am most days.

CHAPTER SEVEN

As middle school loomed before us and Jackie was still in a place emotionally well below his peers, I began to feel sad. His friends were growing up, becoming self-sufficient, secretive, and moody. The onset of puberty was close. Jackie was still nervous about riding his bike to school, still worried about bullies, and excited only about the newest Hot Wheels car. His friends were getting into the video game Five Nights at Freddy's, while he would spend hours with Angry Birds. It was hard to see the gap grow and see how the autism really did affect his behavior. The immaturity and silliness that dominated in third grade was still in charge, and it became annoying to his classmates. Video game night at the local library became the thing to do, but Jackie couldn't be a part of it. Too much stimulation equals too much anger. Kids were hanging out at Subway or the local pizza joint. That was out, too.

Holidays had always been a big deal in my family. Many of my best memories are those of Christmas or Easter: the candy and food of those celebrations or the fun family get-togethers. I wanted to bake cookies with Jackie (not happening), make a huge turkey dinner for him to enjoy (not happening), or eat snow cones on the Fourth of July (not happening). One Christmas, I decided to get him into the mood by taking him to meet Santa in a different way. In our town, there is an old historical house and cabin, built sometime in the mid-1800s. Every Christmas, they have "Dessert with Santa," an old fashioned gathering to show kids what Christmas was like during that time period. At the end, Santa comes out, and since it's a smaller group, everyone gets to see Santa together. I thought this would be perfect until I saw the cabin. It was a small space even for just twelve kids. The open fireplace filled the room with smoke, and there were several oranges hanging above it to dry. One of the projects was to decorate a dried orange with cloves. That was a problem. The close quarters and the smell of orange also became a problem. Jackie held it together until Santa arrived. Santa was tall, bearded, and loud with ringing bells and stomping feet. We had to leave. Santa would never be a good thing in person for Jackie. Since so many of the holiday activities were also anxiety provoking, I decided to focus on Halloween, my favorite of them all. Back in the day, my siblings and I would rummage through the closets, looking for the biggest pillowcases we could find. We'd leave at four in the afternoon only to return when our cases were nearly full. It felt like we were out all night, hunting down our neighborhood friends and filling our faces with candy, but I'm sure we were home by eight. We'd sort through our booty and make trades. I always liked the chewy peanut butter kind that no one else wanted so I always scored big.

I took Jackie trick-or-treating for the first time when he was four. We went about four blocks in the wagon until the giraffe costume became too much. When he was five, he was too afraid to walk to the door, even with a friend, so that ended abruptly as well. Year after year, we tried in vain to fill the plastic pumpkin but got nowhere. The whole thing just terrified him, and the only candy he really liked were M&M's so he just couldn't see the point. As he got older and his friends began to talk about what their costumes would be and how much candy they would get, he began to get a little more interested.

He wanted to be a part of it; he wanted to fit in. So, the fall of fifth grade, I made a plan.

A week before *T-Day,* trick-or-treat day, I printed out a homemade map of the neighborhood and sat Jackie down at the kitchen table.

"OK," I said, as I smoothed out the map. "Here's the plan." He scoured the map with his eyes, a smile beginning to grow. "We hit this street first." I pointed to a street several blocks south. "We'll start at the farthest point and move our way back to our house missing the scary haunted house display here." He sees the area that I'm talking about, the street that has the real live haunted house, complete with character actors and a really big smoke machine. He nods in confirmation. I continue.

"I think we'll be able to cover a lot of ground, but it may take us a few hours. Are you up for that?"

"Yeah," he replies, happily. "We're gonna score this year!"

Yes, we are, I think to myself, *if I have anything to say about it.* Halloween day dawned, and by the time Jackie was home from school, I had the wagon packed: thermoses of milk, a light snack, a blanket, and his Tiggers, plus a Diet Coke for me. His costume was simple, a race car driver with no helmet. I had the plastic pumpkin and another small bag just in case. When he saw it all, his face was full of excitement. The only issue that made me a little worried was the heavy cloud cover quickly approaching, but God wouldn't let it rain. Of course not.

We headed out, and just as we made it to our first door, the rain began to fall.

"It's raining, Mom," Jackie said, with apprehension.

"Nah, this is nothing," I replied, as I hitched a smile on and made light of the heavy drops. "What's a little water? So what if we get a little wet?" I wasn't that convincing, but it wasn't cold out, and toughing it out with the other herds of kids might be fun. Jackie walked to the front door with another group of trick-or-treaters and was excited about the two packets of M&M's that he received. Onward to another house, and then another, and then the rain was coming down faster. Small puddles formed on the sidewalk and streets. Jackie took one wrong step and landed in one, soaking his shoe down to the sock. I saw it on his face—that was it. Three houses were all he could handle. The rain and a fear of lightning, the screaming children splashing in puddles, and the uncomfortable wet sock all added up to sensory overload. It was rough getting back to the house. He began the process of freaking out, angry at the rain, disappointed that the plan had failed, and frustrated that we had begun at the farthest point and now had to hurry home. I pulled his hundred-pound body in the wagon until I thought my arms would fall off. He huddled under the blanket, protecting his Tiggers and screaming for me to hurry. Another Halloween gone bad and the last Halloween that I would take part in. It was a selfish kind of sad that I was feeling. I felt robbed of the childhood that I had dreamed of for my son, robbed of the moments other parents had with their children. I had to remind myself that it wasn't about me, that I was lucky in some ways. I had a child going into middle school soon, a son who still gave me hugs and wanted me around. Other parents were beginning to lose that.

In the fall of sixth grade, the beginning of middle school, it felt like the beginning of a new chapter for Jackie. So when the following Halloween came around, I let him go. He wanted to go trick-or-treating with Alexander and a few other friends. I was a little apprehensive because one of the boys in the group was not always nice to Jackie, but I invited them over to the house to meet up and everything seemed good, so off they went. I had a glimmer of hope that, because Jackie was going with peers, this time would be better. The boys had big plans to fill their bags. Either way, I thought it would be a good experience for him to be out with friends for once and not with his mother. It was time for that. An hour later, the front door opened with a bang, and Jackie came flying in, throwing his large bag of candy to the floor. Alexander came slinking in behind him, looking timid.

"*I hate Halloween!*" Jackie exclaimed. "And I hate those other boys, and Alexander is not my friend!" He began to sob as Alexander stood there, not knowing what to say, again finding himself in the middle of something.

"What happened?" I asked, glancing to each of them.

"That mean kid hit me over the head with his bag of candy, and Alexander didn't even stick up for me!" Of course, there had to be more to the story. He retreated into his bedroom while I drove Alexander home and he filled me in. They had decided to go over to one of the boy's houses after about a half hour of trick-or-treating. Jackie had seen a Hot Wheels car in the boy's bedroom and kept going in to see it even though he had been asked not to. The boy got frustrated and hit Jackie over the head with his bag of candy. I could understand Alexander's hesitation in not sticking up for Jackie, but I could also see, through the eyes of autism, how Jackie felt betrayed. Another bad Halloween and the last time that Jackie would trick-or-treat.

Now, as every holiday comes around, I try to forget my preconceived ideas. I focus on what I know Jackie will like. Not so scary movies in the basement on Halloween with a few friends and lots of ice cream. No trips to see the Easter bunny or Santa, no special cookie baking, and no trips to the old cabin. We have discovered the Santa Tracker online, a website that follows Santa around the world giving quick descriptions of each country and culture. It's educational and somewhat addicting to watch. We set up the computer on Christmas Eve morning, and our day is filled with shout outs of Santa's location at any given moment. That's our tradition. We enjoy the buildup before the holiday as well. Advent calendars, counting down the days, and shopping for the needy are things we look forward to. Using holidays as ways to help others is a big lesson for ASD kids. It's easy for Jackie to be self-centered—and not just on holidays. He is constantly consumed with how any given situation will benefit him. He wants to win every game, have the biggest ice cream, or get the most gifts, and sometimes it's difficult for him to show empathy, but it's there. If a friend is hurting, he's the first one there, telling him that things will be OK. He refuses the drive into the city because he can't stand to see any homeless people. He will cry buckets whenever he sees those commercials for impoverished African families or animals that have been abused. But on holidays, especially, he just wants stuff. We're working on it.

CHAPTER EIGHT

As Jackie headed into middle school, I noticed a switch in his behavior. Though he suffered from anxiety and anger issues, the anger piece was beginning to escalate, and more often than not, a day would end with meltdowns. My afternoons were filled with Jackie's crying over a frustrating day, anger over being forced to sit through a band concert when it wasn't even on the schedule, or anxiety over homework from a substitute teacher. The pressures of growing up were taking their toll, and the loosening of structure was playing a big part in it all. Middle school was designed to give more freedoms, more challenges, and to help push children into independence, all things that he just wasn't ready for.

One evening, after a particularly stressful day, he was so full of anger that he did something I never saw coming. We were in his bedroom, and he was getting ready to call it a day and hit the sack early. My mother's voice would echo in my head as I remembered my own childhood. If I was ever crabby or talking back, she would automatically say, *Oh, Diane, you're just tired.* That would get her, of course, an eye roll from me, thinking that she didn't understand anything. Now it has become my solution to angry or sad afternoons and, I have to say, she was right. It works sometimes. Jackie was upset about going to bed an hour before his normal time, and as I was beginning to explain the reasoning behind my decision, I saw his arm pull back out of the corner of my eye. As I turned toward him, that arm loaded with a closed fist came swinging into my back. Physical contact. We had now reached that incredibly scary point that many ASD parents deal with. Because kids on the spectrum are very reactive, unable to stop and think before they react, violence to themselves and others can be an issue. I looked at Jackie as his face crumbled and tears began to stream down his face. I looked at his five-foot, two-inch frame, and thought, *This can't happen again.* I envisioned Jackie at fifteen. I saw a six-foot young man pulling that same arm back, unable to control his anger, and I freaked out on the inside.

He fell into my arms. "I'm sorry," he sobbed. "I'm so sad." It was time to have the first of many difficult talks, and I knew that I had to be firm.

"I know you don't want to hurt me," I said. "And I'm not hurt at all." He glanced up at me, making sure I was OK. "The thing is, Jackie, you can't let your anger out by hitting people, not even me."

"I won't do it again," he replied. He looked terrified. "I just got so mad."

"That's a problem, especially if you felt like you couldn't control it."

"It's not my fault!" he yelled. "You made me go to bed early." That's wasn't good. The blame game is never good.

"I know you're upset about that, but there is never a reason to hit anyone. If you hit me, and I get hurt, you'll end up in juvy and, believe me, you'll never make it in there."

"You would send me to juvy?" He had recently learned about *juvy* from covertly watching a YouTube video of *Scared Straight*. I hadn't been happy about his watching something so violent without my permission, but now, at least he had real proof that juvy existed.

"Yes, I'd have to. I can't live with a son who I'm afraid will hurt me." That was it. He began to cry again, this time remorsefully. I felt a little heart-less threatening to send him to jail, but he needed to know the truth, and that would be a real conse-quence if he became violent.

"I know that tonight you just didn't know how to show how angry you were. We can come up with a better way, OK?" And that's what we did. The Hit Pillow was created, and I kind of felt sorry for it. Still, better it than me. We also came up with a strategy for overwhelming days when anger ruled. If he felt as if he were going to be angry to the point of becoming out of control, he needed to go to his bedroom. I stressed that this was not a punishment but instead a safe place to calm down and maybe give Hit Pillow a go. The first time that I suggested he go to his room to calm down, he did so, stomping all the way up the stairs. I even got a few door slams, but soon enough, he began to go on his own. To this day, he has never acted violent toward me or anyone else that I know of. The anger is still there and explosive at times, but short lived. Dealing with it is a work in progress. Still, anger can be a real problem with ASD children, and the solutions are not always this simple.

The bigger issue from all of this was that Jackie was struggling at school. The teachers painted a pic-ture that just wasn't reality. He was too young to ad-vocate for himself. I couldn't go on handling all the baggage that was loaded on him every day. So I began a weekly e-mail correspondence with the teachers and social worker, giving them the low down on what emotional state Jackie was in at home. Together we began to figure out the causes by looking at each school day. This allowed the social worker to home in on problems before Jackie brought them home. It took a lot of stress off me and began to teach Jackie how to advocate for himself. The main thing that I wanted the school to understand was that things are not always what they seem. With ASD kids, you cannot assume anything. You can't think that they understand just because they don't say anything. You can't think that they are unaffected just because they seem to be fine. There needs to be constant communication between educators and the child, as well as between educators and parents. It takes a village after all, and many of Jackie's teachers have told me how much easier it is for them because of this open communication. They understand him in ways that they might not have otherwise. That's big to me because all I really want for him is to be under-stood, not only at school but also in all of his social relationships.

At about this time, when the anger issue was growing, Jackie began to do some serious talking back. I would ask him to get ready for bed only to be told that he would get ready when he wanted to. My first response to this was to throttle him, grab his iPad, and stomp on it, but of course, that wouldn't solve anything. I tried to explain the importance of being a better listener, how if he didn't get enough sleep he wouldn't be ready for school in the morning. I even suggested that on the weekend we could decide on a later bedtime if he really wanted to stay up. After giving him a five-minute warning he replied, "Yeah, right Mom, like I'm actually listening."

"Jackie, I need you to get ready now." I had had enough.

"Get over it." He continued to watch his YouTube car videos. That had been his first choice in response lately...*Get over it.* I sat in my room, thinking about how best to handle this whole thing. It felt like his talking back and the inability to listen and follow direction were getting worse. A part of me understood that, really, this was his way of trying to be grown up and independent. He wanted to set his own rules. I decided to turn the tables on him, show him what it felt like to be spoken to in such an unfeeling way. So I told him that I was going to bed and that he could put himself to bed. That kind of freaked him out, but he said OK. I still have no idea what time he actually went to sleep that night, but when he got up for school the next morning he was exhausted.

In our hurry to get everything together and head out the door, he asked, "Mom, can you find my sports book so I can take it to school?"

"No, we have to leave now. I don't have time to dig through your books right now."

"But, Mom, I really need it today!" he whined.

I looked him square in the eye and said, "Get over it." He was startled. "You should have spent that extra awake time finding it."

This went on for a few days.

"Mom, I need help!"

At first, Jackie tried to brush it off, acting as if my *Get over it* response didn't bother him at all. Then one night he was asking for a snack, and when I said that I couldn't possibly get him a snack because my fingers hurt and he should just get over the fact that he wanted a snack, he smiled.

"OK, Mom. I get it," he said. I came to sit next to him on his bed.

"You know, Jackie, there are rules for you to follow because they make sense. I'm sure you were tired the other day when you decided to stay up later than normal." He nodded. "I'm happy to talk about the rules that you think are bad and maybe even compromise a little, but not when you talk to me with disrespect."

"I felt like you didn't care about me when you talked to me like you did."

"That's how I felt, too." Lesson learned.

I have found with Jackie that sometimes the best way for him to learn a lesson is through example. He needs to experience the consequences himself to really understand what his actions do to others. He is also a follower. If one of his peers is swearing in the locker room, then in his mind, it must be OK. He knows that swearing is something that I don't want him to do, but as with most tweens and teens, believes that I couldn't possibly understand that swearing is what they do and that it's OK. If a teacher were to bust him for swearing, he wouldn't be able to understand it unless everyone that he's heard utter a swear word at school were also in trouble. The idea that one person could get in trouble for something that others do is foreign and unfair to him. That kind of mind-set makes for a messy life. It's something that I continue to talk about.

CHAPTER NINE

I magine standing in a small room filled with other people, all bumping into you, each voice raised, each voice having a different conversation, sometimes in languages you can't understand. Add in a dead skunk, rancid milk, and a wire poking into the back of your neck. Do you think you'd be happy? Would it be easy to carry on a conversation with the person next to you, the guy standing on your foot, and the guy holding the wire that's poking you? Could you pay attention to one person, hear his conversation above the noise of everyone else? Would you be nice, happy, or calm? This is what every day looks like for many ASD kids. This was Jackie early on. I don't think he was really aware of the craziness because that was all he knew; but at the onset of middle school, this internal struggle manifested big time.

Jackie has always been a hard loser. It was impossible to play board games as he grew up. The minute that he thought he was losing, there would be blame on the other player, accusations of cheating, and the throwing of the board as the pieces went flying. He wanted to make up his own rules. That sometimes worked if everyone was on board with what he wanted to do, but not always. Black and white: winning is good; losing is bad. So to help him with this issue, I decided to see if chess club was an option. He took to the game immediately. It's the one place where he can be in his mind and nobody cares. With his mind, he learned quickly and soon was one of the leading players on the team. He still had a difficult time losing, but it was all for fun, and he was making new friends so he wanted to keep at it.

In middle school, we decided that it was time to begin playing chess in tournaments. If you've ever been involved in the chess community, this is no joke. Chess is serious business, not a game, but a way of life. I was amazed at our first tournament to see a tiny first grader sitting across from an adult, ready to take on the challenge even while squirming in his seat. Jackie was nervous and rightly so, but excited. I saw him eyeing the trophies, and my stomach fell a little. I knew it would be difficult for him to leave empty-handed. Unfortunately, that's exactly what happened on that day. He lost every game. We were not prepared for this level of play, and he was crushed. He stomped out of the tournament screaming and crying, full of anger, and feeling as if he might never be good enough. I looked at him and waited for him to calm down.

"I know that it's hard not to win," I said as we sat in the car. "You have every right to be disappointed."

"I never want to play chess again!" he spat, wiping his eyes.

"You never have to if you really don't want to," I replied. He seemed surprised. "This is for you, not for me. It should be fun, and if it isn't, then let's not do it." He thought about this, and I could tell he was torn. These people, the chess people, were his people. He knew this the minute he began to learn the game—kids deep in thought, cerebral. He didn't want to give that up, but it hurt to lose.

"So, here's the deal," I continued. "If you still want to play, I'll do everything in my power to help you get better. We'll hire a coach, you can work on the game on a different level, and we'll come back to this tournament in a few months, and you can kick butt." A smile was playing at the corner of his lips.

"Yeah, OK, let's do that,"

Of course the first thing that our new coach said to Jackie was, "You have to lose games to get better." This was tough to hear and still is to this day. But after several months of lessons, we did go back to that tournament, and Jackie walked out with the fifth place trophy. Since then, he has won more than thirty chess trophies, and the game has been a good way to teach him that losing isn't always bad. But just when I thought that lesson was sinking in, we had a major step back.

It was a new tournament; something that I thought would be exciting. I wanted to give Jackie some new blood to battle on the board. But as we walked into the building and down to the tournament hall, I knew things were not going to go well. It was loud and crazy with kids running everywhere, knocking over tables, and spilling their drinks. If you've never been a part of the chess-tournament scene, you might not realize the difficulty. Usually tournaments are silent. The kids are led into a separate space where numbered boards are set up and there is absolutely no talking. Parents are not allowed in to watch but instead have their own waiting room. This has always worked out well for Jackie. The quiet helps him concentrate and stay focused.

So when I saw the chaos going on around us in this new tournament, I almost turned us around and left. I thought that there was no way that Jackie could win with all the noise. Internally, he would be racing. The tournament directors were also allowing parents and siblings to watch and were not quieting anyone. In the heat of the tournament, brothers and sisters raced around the tables and called out to one another, while parents talked in the background. There was someone boiling hot dogs somewhere, and the room had a carnival odor to match the atmosphere. I watched as Jackie concentrated on his first opponent and the pieces in front of him. Surprisingly, he won his first game and then his second. After four long, loud hours, he had won three and lost one. I knew that he would be a contender for a trophy, but I wasn't sure how he would place. When it was all over, he was revved up inside, his body now reacting to the outside stimulus. He had a short fuse and was complaining about everything. We held on while the rest of the games finished up and it was finally trophy time. He had no idea where he had placed. There were three huge trophies and two smaller trophies displayed on the table in front of us. The first place trophy was topped with a golden cup, very impressive, and something that I knew Jackie had dreamed of—a trophy with a golden cup. When the directors began reading off the winners, Jackie sat waiting, glancing over to me after each name was read. Fifth place, not Jackie. Fourth place, not Jackie. Third place, not Jackie. I saw that he was nervous and beginning to think that he might not have done as well as he thought. His head began to hang when second place was announced and his name was called. The smile was from ear to ear. Who cared about a big golden cup when the second place trophy was just as ginormous and belonged to him. He held it up as the first-place winner was announced. As the golden cup was handed to the winner, another boy whispered to Jackie, "Hey, you beat that guy. You should get the first place trophy!" I saw the confusion all over his face, but I knew that that's not how it worked. Though Jackie may have played the golden cup winner and even won against him, the trophy winners weren't chosen based solely on that. It can be confusing, and generally the tournament directors have the whole thing computerized using many different criteria. Unfortunately, the woman handing out the trophies didn't understand this, and hearing that Jackie had beaten the golden cup winner in his round, she quickly gave Jackie the first place trophy and gave his second place one to the winner. My stomach dropped as I saw the look of pride all over my son's face, and I knew that I'd be the one to crush him. Pictures were taken, and Jackie wandered over to the tables to get into a pick-up game. The directors approached me, and I knew what they were about to say. They began to explain how the process worked, and I held up a hand to stop them.

"Yeah, I know," I said. "It's just unfortunate that the first place trophy was handed to him. I'll explain it and we can switch out the trophies." *How do I explain that?* I thought. It's a done deal in Jackie's mind. After all, they wouldn't give him the trophy if he hadn't won it fair and square. Black and white, no room for mistakes. I decided to approach the whole thing like ripping off a Band-Aid, quickly and hopefully with the least amount of pain. I took the second place trophy and walked over to where Jackie sat, deep in thought, with the golden cup perched next to him, and quickly make the switch. The first place winner ran off just as Jackie looked at me and asked me what I was doing. I explained it all to him, the mistake that the woman made and the fact that he won second place and wasn't that great! *Redirect, redirect, redirect…*

"Now let's get a picture of you with this awesome trophy, and then we can go out for ice cream to celebrate!" Slowly he stood, his eyes wandering across the room, searching for the golden cup.

"Where is it?" he yelled at the top of his lungs. "Where's my trophy?" I huddled next to him, whispering in his ear, "No, Jackie. This is your trophy." I could almost see the steam and fire coming out of his ears as he began to pound on the table, screaming repeatedly.

"They're cheaters! That's my trophy! I beat that guy! Everyone is cheating! I want my trophy!" For the first time, there was quiet as every face turned to us. There were small children whose hands were empty while my son complained about the huge second place trophy next to him. Other mothers gave me the eye, and fathers shook their heads. What poor sportsmanship, what a bad example to the younger kids who were walking away with nothing. I did the only thing that a mother could do in this kind of situation. I grabbed my son by the arm with one hand, snatched the trophy from the table with the other, and pulled them both out the door and away from the scene. The complaining didn't stop in the car. He was indignant, outraged, and didn't even want the trophy sitting in the backseat. All I could think about was how different this day would have ended if that woman had simply not switched the trophies and if that boy had not said anything. Still, if I'm honest with myself, a typical child might have been upset at first, but in the end would have been able to see the mistake, and would have been OK with second place. Jackie's response was intense, long lasting, and completely unfiltered.

The anger lasted the whole way home and dissolved into sadness and tears the rest of the night. I have revisited this event many, many times, trying to explain it over and over again. Even today, when Jackie knows how tournaments work and how tiebreakers are figured out, if you ask him about that tournament, he'll tell you that they cheated. He cannot see through the fact that the first place trophy was in his hands. Since then, he has won a first place trophy with a golden cup, and I think that helps a little. He has also lost many tournaments with little complaint, but I can't forget the looks on the other parents' faces from that awful day. I wish that I could have explained it all to them—his reaction and where it came from. I wish that I could have told them that the loud noise and the crazy atmosphere had been a precursor to his explosion. That event was the first time that I had that awful, sick feeling in the pit of my gut, the feeling of being judged, the feeling that maybe I was a bad parent, or that maybe I was wrong to let him act the way that he did. But, really, what were my choices? You can't force a child to understand something that his brain is just not capable of understanding. It was definitely time for me to toughen up.

After that episode, there were many more like it, and not only with chess. As Jackie got older and taller, it became easier for outsiders to look at him and make negative assumptions about his behavior. It became more commonplace for teachers to forget the ASD and the positive way to speak to Jackie. They forgot how to help him understand the deep feelings of things being unjust that he seemed always to dwell on. Thank goodness for the school social workers. They were key in his progress, even in the face of teachers who didn't always get it.

CHAPTER TEN

Middle school had been a real fear. The kids looked so big to me, so old. This was the first time for classroom changes during the day, with a new classroom and teacher for each subject. There were new kids, maybe even kids who climbed the social ladder by stepping on the weak or different. As sixth grade progressed for Jackie, all of my own middle-school drama came back to haunt me in a full flood of emotion. I was different then, the kid who couldn't read, the kid who was chubby, introverted, and not at all smart. I remembered how important the social game was, how it felt like the end of the world sitting alone at lunch, or feeling how desperately I wanted to fit in with the popular group. It all seems so meaningless now, but I knew that was the path Jackie was embarking on, and I was afraid for him.

I sat down for the transitional IEP meeting wondering what accommodations could be made to protect him from the angst of it all, knowing that he would have to learn his lessons just as I had. It never ceased to amaze me how everyone at the IEP meetings seemed to think that we were on a path to no accommodations and that there was always someone saying, "Wouldn't it be great if in a year or two we could not have a need for an IEP anymore?" I mean, I've already looked into colleges and what they supply in the way of help for students with ASD. I don't know why it rubs me the wrong way. Maybe I feel as if everyone thinks that ASD goes away over time, or maybe it's this idea that somehow my child should be made to fit in, or that others seem always to want to downplay it all. It's that same idea that what you see is what you get with Jackie, when that couldn't be further from the truth. Believe me, I wished that he fit in better. There were so many times that I looked at his peers, saw how much they had matured, how much they were able to handle, and I choked back tears. I wondered what Jackie would be like without ASD; would he be like his friends—calm, cool, and a part of everything? So, I sat, listened, and then pushed for accommodations, such as a resource hour for decompression during the day or social group meetings once a week. The one thing that we all agree on is Jackie's need to accommodate for himself. That's the big goal; letting people know when he needs help. So right before middle school, we added a list of things that might be needed—just in case—with the idea that we could cross them off if they were never needed. We crossed a lot off after that first year.

I dropped Jackie off at his new school one day with butterflies in my stomach. I could tell that he was nervous, too, but there was also a sense of pride in his stance, a sense of *I'm growing up* that made him feel special. I went with that as I pushed the butterflies down. Not many people know this, but I had a spy within the school, a good family friend who worked in the lunchroom. She would text me if she noticed anything, filling me in on the dynamic. So far, things had looked good. He was sitting with Alexander at lunch and he seemed happy. That day, when I picked him up from school, he rattled on about the day. He had hung out with several friends that were in his classes, his teachers seemed nice, the lunchroom smelled, and it was loud in the hallways.

"And guess what else happened?" he said with such enthusiasm that I was sure they were handing out toy cars as well.

"What?" I replied happily, innocently.

"The boys in the locker room were swearing and I did, too!"

Huh?

"Really?"

"Yeah, it was so cool!" He turned to me, a big smile on his face as if swearing were the greatest thing in the world. *Too much information. Way too much information.* I tried not to overreact. After all, this is what I get all the time, uncensored truth.

"Wow," I replied. "That's, that's, um…"

"It was cool," he finished for me.

"OK, but just so you know, if an adult ever hears you say those words, you could get into big trouble. It's probably better to listen and not join in." Unfortunately, swearing would become a big problem later on.

Though swearing in the locker room was cool, he did have some anxiety with his hallway locker, and he felt as if there wasn't enough time to get from class to class. We fixed that with an accommodation to leave his books in a bin in a classroom so that he could just swing by and pick them up as he needed them. Though things seemed positive that first week, I felt—mother's intuition—that there was something he wasn't telling me. I left it alone at first, not wanting to ruin the positivity. Then on Friday, as he got into the car, he spilled it.

"Mom, I'm not sure if this is a bad thing or not, but something's happening in gym class."

"Really? What is it?" I asked, hoping for the best.

"Well, during the week, a few kids kept stealing my gym locker lock so I couldn't lock up my clothes. I was afraid that if they took the lock that I would get in trouble for losing it."

"Oh, that doesn't sound very nice." I tried to keep my voice steady. I didn't want to show how incredibly upset I was getting. I guessed that the swearing kids might not be so cool after all. "What did you do?"

"Well, I put the lock in my underwear so that they couldn't take it."

"So you went to gym class with your lock in your underwear?"

"Yeah, but then today I came back to my locker after class and my clothes were gone." *Freaking out, freaking out, freaking out…*

"What happened?" My voice was completely unsteady now.

"My friend found them in the garbage."

"Did you tell the teacher?"

"Yes, and he said he would talk to the boys that did it."

Casually I asked, "Oh, good. What are their names?"

This was the horrible incident that I had been worried about. The thing that made it ten times worse was that Jackie wasn't even sure if he had been bullied or not. I thought about how he might be put in these kinds of situations repeatedly because he was so trusting and naive, and I was sick. The boy's locker room is the notorious place where it all begins, the banter and flexing. Boys talking smack about private parts, or name calling, or clothes stealing, all in the name of claiming the alpha role. It's generally accepted in our society—even expected—and laughed off. If I have to hear one more time about how this is all typical for middle schoolers, I'll strongly consider home schooling. To me it's all crazy. To accept certain behaviors simply because it's common to the age is ridiculous. So I called the principal first and wrote a letter to the editor of the *Chicago Tribune* second. I wanted to make it all public, let people know my outrage, at least.

More and more, I was beginning to understand that all the things I was fighting for to help Jackie were also the things that would help kids in general. The issue wasn't just autism; it was the lack of kindness and understanding within the school system, as well as within the community. The idea of taking time to get to know someone, listening to his or her ideas or issues, and showing respect—these are concepts seemingly lost for children. Yet how do children learn best other than by example? Still, I doubted myself, and I knew that other parents, probably a greater percentage than not, wouldn't agree with me.

In this instance, the boys admitted their actions to the principal and apologized, saying that they knew it was wrong but that it all kind of just snowballed. As usual, Jackie accepted their apologies, and there was never an issue like this again. That may have been mostly because of my insistence that an adult be present in the locker room at all times, or the fact that my letter was published in the newspaper within the next few weeks, who knows? But this was just the beginning of the obstacles that middle school and puberty would bring. I thought I was ready for it, but I sure wasn't.

CHAPTER ELEVEN

It was clear, as time went on, that the gap between Jackie and his peers was growing even bigger. Jackie's interests remained deep in Hot Wheels, and cars in general, and that interest was pretty much it. He began to lose some of the friends whom he had been close to in elementary school as their interests leaned to sports or techy stuff that Jackie just wasn't into. It was hard for him to connect with anyone new, especially with kids who didn't know about his ASD. It became a daily ritual for at least one person to call him annoying because he couldn't stop talking about a certain subject or couldn't tell when people were tired of his attempts to be funny. His self-esteem began to fall, and we moved into that moody, dark place of adolescence.

I tried to encourage Jackie to join a club. Alexander was in Tech Club, and Jackie tried that for a while, but it didn't stick. Then he saw a flyer for Science Olympiad. He had another friend who had already joined, and so that was all it took for him. The team met one day a week after school, and after the first meeting, it seemed as if it would be a positive thing in his life. He had always been science minded, and I thought that maybe this team might help him to not only make new friends but also broaden an existing interest. But by the fourth week, things began to look fishy. I picked him up, and he threw his backpack into the backseat and slammed the door shut hard.

"What's wrong?" I asked in surprise.

"I'm never going back to Science Olympiad!" More shock.

"What happened?"

"Those kids in there are bullying me!" Oh no. Not again! I couldn't believe it. I knew most of the kids on the team. They were good kids, nice kids.

"Who's bullying you?" I asked, wondering if it might be the older kids, the eighth graders who looked more like high schoolers to me. He said that it was.

"We have our first competition next weekend, and they are telling me that I'm lazy and that I shouldn't go." That got me a little upset, but it also got me wondering about what goes on in that classroom after school.

"Well, have you been working on something to present?" Silence.

"I don't know what to work on."

Clearly, there was a bigger problem. I wondered if this club might not be right for Jackie, especially with the older kids calling him out. I decided to e-mail the teacher who was in charge and get her input. I'm glad I did. What I discovered changed the way that I looked at Jackie's interpretation of certain events in his life. It was the beginning of realizing that his perceptions might be tainted by his ASD, and that *his* reality might not always match true reality.

After typing an e-mail detailing the bullying accusations, the problem with Jackie's project, and his feelings of confusion about the club, I asked her if this club was right for him. She assured me that it was. She assured me that there had not been any bullying and that Jackie seemed fine in the classroom. It was confusing. How could the two accounts of Science Olympiad be so different? I did the only thing that I could think of and decided to be a volunteer coach. I wanted to see the problems for myself, before Jackie gave up a team that really would fit him. I was also ready to see the bullies in action.

But on that first day when I entered the science classroom, I became enlightened. I stood in the doorway in horror as kids came rushing in and out, throwing their backpacks to the floor where they became obstacles blocking the path to the white-boards. The noise level was deafening, and no one seemed to be working on anything. It was total cha-os to me, so I could just imagine what it was like for Jackie. Kids were grouped around tables, checking their phones, playing video games, with a select few seemingly doing research or building some kind of contraption. And there was Jackie, out of con-trol, jumping from table to table, stealing iPads or phones left unprotected. It was a game to him. He would snatch a device and run for the hallway. The device's owner would jump up and race after him. It began as a joke, with both sides laughing, but af-ter a few minutes, the joke was over and ended up with an angry kid yelling for his phone while Jackie continued to run. He was fast, too, so fast that the chaser usually gave up and went back into the room mumbling something about being annoyed. Jackie would return, continuing to taunt, only to be con-fused as to why the game was over or why he was being called annoying.

Whoa!

Then he'd turn to someone else and try it again. He was hyped up, the loud and crazy environment churning around inside of him, egging him on. He couldn't stop. I tried to take him by the arm, but he ran from me. He couldn't hear me calling him because of the noise in the room and the noise in his head. I turned to the teacher, who seemed unfazed.

"So what is it that Jackie should be working on?" I asked. She handed me a pile of papers.

"He'll be doing the Dynamic Planet event as well as Wind Power. Here is the information."

"Has he begun any of the work?" I asked. She looked at me questioningly.

"Well, he can do the building at home, or he can bring in materials to do the work here." She paused as if confused. "I did give him the instructions, and he seemed excited about it. Most of the kids do the majority of the work at home and then work with their partners here to get everything organized." I took another glance around the room as a water bottle went flying by.

"I can tell you that nothing will get done here," I replied. "He's completely out of control." I explained to her that this environment was too much for him and that, generally, he couldn't work independently unless he was given direct instructions. A few sheets of paper wouldn't do it. The teacher was very understanding. Apparently, she had thought that Jackie had been working on the projects at home. She had assumed that he understood the plan. I could now see why the older kids had thought he was lazy. I could understand their annoyance. And now I could help fix it. I took Jackie out of the classroom and found a quiet place to go over the projects. We looked at the building of the fan for Wind Power and broke it down into steps and then planning time to actually do the work. Now he was getting excited. I went back to the classroom and got to know some of the older kids, and they were really cool, really smart, and not bullies at all. I began to realize that Jackie was the cause of much irritation, even though he really didn't mean to be. He just wanted to fit in.

On that first competition day, not only did we bring his projects but also the chessboard and set it up in our homeroom to entertain everyone between events. As Jackie beat every opponent, even the eighth graders, I saw a glimmer of respect begin to grow from his peers.

"I don't know if you know this," I said to one of the older boys, right after he lost his third round. "But Jackie has autism, and that's why he can be so good at chess." Several of the other older kids heard me and glanced my way.

"I didn't know that," the boy replied.

"Yeah, and it's also why he has a hard time knowing when to stop trying to be funny. It can be annoying, but all you have to do is tell him in a serious voice that you need him to stop,"

That was the beginning of Science Olympiad being a good fit for Jackie. He won a medal that day and continued to go on for another year and win many more. Both years that he participated, the team made it to state. It opened up a door for meeting new friends, but it took a summer of movies, amusement parks, and pool time with them to really solidify the friendships. Everyone was so supportive, both the teacher and the other students. It brought back my faith in people, something that I had lost along the way.

In the early years, I was naïve. I thought that once my community knew about my son's diagnosis, people would come forward to help. I believed that those around me, the parents of the children whom we knew, the educators who surrounded us, and the friends whom I had made along the way, would rally and begin the process of understanding. So when I reached out to other parents, asking them to teach their children about autism and how best to talk to Jackie, and I got an *I don't care* sort of response, I was heartbroken. People had their own lives, their own problems to deal with, and, understandably, few had little time for anything else. This was at a time when autism was just starting to appear in the media. The buzz was starting but hadn't swept the country yet. A few came forward. They were the friends and teachers who had a connection somewhere else with ASD, and that was comforting, but I was sad, angry, and alone. I longed for other children who would take Jackie by the hand and show him right from wrong, show him that they would always be his friends, and help him navigate the social arena. Science Olympiad did that in a small way, and my heart began to heal. I realized that as his peers got older, they would begin to understand better the things that Jackie struggled with. I pinned my hopes on that. I still do.

But, even as Jackie got older, his maturity remained at a much lower level than his peers' maturity. In middle school, his main interest was still cars, Hot Wheels, sports cars, and that was it. As hard as I tried to open up his mind to new interests, nothing ever really stuck. So recently, I took him to his first Hot Wheels convention. He was in his glory, chatting it up with other kids and adults, discussing the newest cases and Hot Wheels Treasure Hunts that were available. At the back of the room was a long table set up for autographs. As I scanned the names on the sign next to the table, I had no idea who these people were. I discovered quickly that they were all Hot Wheels designers, and my heart raced. If I couldn't expand Jackie's mind, I would take the passion that he already had and figure out a way for it to be the biggest part of his life as an adult. What better job could there be for him than working for Mattel and the Hot Wheels brand some day? I picked the designers' brains, asking questions about getting started in a career like theirs. It turned out that Jackie was already on the right path: engineering and design of cars. I brought Jackie over and introduced him to the designers, and they let me take a picture of Jackie sitting behind the signing table with them. After we left, I told Jackie about their jobs, and he was sold. I guess we'll see. One wish we all have as parents is that our children have a career someday that they love. And the best part about this job is that he could be himself, focused on the computer screen, in his head, building what he loves, all day long.

CHAPTER TWELVE

With some maturity, I truly believed that the sensory issues, especially the food issues that Jackie faced, would dissipate. I could envision him as a teenager, sitting with his friends in McDonald's, chomping on a cheeseburger, talking smack about how horrible the newest Chevy model was. Unfortunately, though I did see growth in middle school, the food issues continued. It was difficult for him to sit at the dinner table every night. The smell or look of the food bothered him that much. It became a huge source of drama between him and his father, putting me in the middle most of the time. His father wanted to sit with him, talk about his day, and connect on a certain level.

Jackie, overwhelmed by the food and by being questioned, was unable to meet him there, unable to hide his feelings of annoyance. It was a real struggle and not unusual for a family with a special needs child. I think his father longed for that special father and son relationship that as a parent you dream about. I think he hoped that, over time, the ASD would go away or become less noticeable, and it was hard when that didn't happen. It was hard for me, too. It truth, it's so much better if both parents are on the same page in parenting, but that just can't always happen, so I did my best to try to understand both sides—Jackie's and his father's—and kept trying to get them to meet in the middle.

I love a good road trip. Jackie's pretty easy to travel with after you get past the cooler packed with the only foods he'll eat and the gallons of whole milk. As long as he has his iPad, it doesn't really matter how long we're in the car. My father, who now lives in Illinois, is from Minnesota, and so every summer we try to go back and visit all the relatives who are still there. It's a relatively easy drive, somewhere around seven hours from our house on the North Shore, and we try to make at least one stop to stretch our legs and have a bathroom break. Jackie and I love a good truck stop, the kind that has just about every-thing, from tree-shaped car air fresheners, to a bin of stuffed animals, to a shower station for the truck-ers. For my parents, it's more about the breakfast stop, and so we always try to make it as comfortable as we can for Jackie.

He has a tendency to freak out in new restau-rants, because of the smells, the noise, and the strange food sitting on the table in front of him. He can usually do a pancake. I always feel that it must give him a sense of belonging to be able to eat out occasionally, to be able to fit into that environment occasionally. On one particular trip, we chose a Cracker Barrel restaurant, knowing that Jackie loved the gift shop there and that, in the past, this had been an OK place for him. We got as far as the gift shop when Jackie began to panic. It seemed to come out of nowhere, and as we were led to our table by the hostess, he lost it completely.

"I can't stay here. I can't stay here. I can't stay here..."

"Jackie, tell me what's bothering you. We could ask for a table next to the window so that you can watch the traffic come in and out." I was grasping at ways to fix it. I just wanted us to be able to enjoy our meal and the trip together.

"OK," he replied, and we quickly were reseated. It didn't help. The waitress took our order and set a tall glass of milk down in front of Jackie. His eyes darted around the room to the other patrons. He glanced at the milk. "I can't stay here," he said again.

"It's OK," I replied. "Just try your milk, and we'll leave as soon as we eat. Then we can check out the gift shop." A little bribe never hurt. He got louder in his protest, as he stood to his full six-foot-frame height, and accusations flew.

"Why did you bring me here? I hate this place! The food stinks!" My poor parents. They had their own look of fear and confusion, and, waiting for a resolution, they both fixed their eyes on me. Jackie's protests continued as I tried to reason it out with him, tried to understand why, this time, it was so difficult. I glanced over my shoulder and saw an older couple watching; the man shook his head in disgust, and the woman leaned in, whispering to him across the table. They wouldn't stop staring, and I knew what they were thinking. The man looked like he was ready to stand up, grab Jackie by the arm, and pull him from the restaurant. All I could think about was how much I wanted to grab the man and bash his head against the wall. How much I wanted to take him by the collar of his starched white shirt and shake him for not understanding. I wanted to scream, *Look, my son has autism, and he can't handle restaurants sometimes, and this is one of those times, so just turn around and ignore us, please, because, really, he can't help it!* This is my fault. I should have just let him stay in the car. I just wanted him to have that normalcy for once. But maybe it was more for me. I'm not a violent person. I felt bad for having those thoughts about the couple who clearly misjudged the situation, but sometimes the whole autism thing just pushes you over the edge.

I have a friend whose mother is suffering from Alzheimer's. Sometimes when they go to a restaurant, her mother will roam to other tables and try to talk to the strangers there. Because of this, my friend had some cards printed. They say, "My mother has Alzheimer's. I'm sorry if she is bothering you. Please try to be understanding." She told me that it might make it easier if I also ordered cards. I thought, *Is this what the world has come to? Do I actually have to hand out autism cards to get people to be tolerant, kind, and patient?* Not doing it. My parents were so kind, volunteering to leave and hit a drive through instead, but that wasn't the right solution. I ended up finding a nice rocking chair right outside of our window for Jackie to sit in and wait for us until we were done. He was still agitated, but the relief was palpable as he saw us exit the restaurant. It turned out that Jackie had had a bad experience at another Cracker Barrel with his father. That would have been nice to know *before* we had made the stop. As for the staring couple, as I walked by their table on my way out I softly said,

"Autism can be a very difficult thing." I'm not sure how they took that, but given the chance to educate others, I take it.

This situation wasn't the first time that I received *the look* from people around me. It began early on in Jackie's diagnosis. The terrible trips to Target where tantrums over unnecessary wants occurred; the terrible-two tantrums being played out by a tall third grader; waiting in line for an hour for a picture with Santa, only to experience a total meltdown just as it's our turn, a meltdown that included an exclamation that the man in the white beard is fake anyway. The screaming that he can't go into church because it burns him and that he'd rather go to hell than sit through a church service. Everything is over the top; everything that is seemingly small to me as a rational human being is so big to him. And the looks from other people only made me want to hide. In the early days, I would come home from a shopping trip with Jackie and just cry. I could handle him. I could figure out eventually what might have set him off in a particular situation, and I could fix it. But I couldn't fix what others were thinking, and that hurt. In those early days, I was constantly worried that I was somehow doing all of this, making the autism happen. It took years of *the look* to finally say *I don't care*, and that changed everything. That was the beginning of changing my focus from what others thought of Jackie to what Jackie thought of himself, and making sure that he was OK with it all.

The restaurant issues and tantrums are now few and far between. As Jackie got older, he slowly began to advocate for himself. He also began to know when there could be situations that might make him feel uncomfortable and found ways to deal with them. Recently, his class was scheduled to take a field trip into the city. They were going to a restaurant to experience foods of different cultures. When Jackie told me about it, he prefaced the conversation by stating that he didn't want to go because he knew that it would make him uncomfortable. Not only would the sensory issues be a problem, but also he was at the age where the whole thing was embarrassing. We made plans to go to a movie that day, instead. He was a little sad about his choice not to attend the field trip. The consequence of his choice was that he missed out on time with his friends outside the classroom. But this will be his life, making choices that are best for him when dealing with his autism. I was relieved that he was making the choice for himself and that now I wouldn't have to deal with the backlash of overstimulation had he attended the restaurant event. And I liked this new way of life; I liked not having to be constantly in the middle of it all. As Jackie matured in middle school, the issues of autism didn't go away. They didn't even get better necessarily. They just changed. Now, we were dealing with many more social issues, and the sensory stuff was fading into the background. Now we were worrying about girls, friends, feelings of depression, and much, much more anger. And my problem centered around deciphering the true reality from Jackie's. In light of the Science Olympiad situation, I knew that sometimes Jackie was the one creating the problem, but certainly not always.

I try to keep relationships with the friends and peers that Jackie knows. There are a special handful of kids that I call my Peeps. They fill me in on the drama that happens during the school day, and they are good kids, kids that I've known since kindergarten. When I opened my e-mail one evening and saw a message from a schoolmate that wasn't in my Peeps list, I was concerned. The e-mail was desperate. The young lady, Mia, was a girl in one of Jackie's classes and a mutual friend of Alexander. I had heard her name before because there had been some conflict between her and Jackie. Apparently, Alexander had wanted to spend time with Mia during lunch. Jackie had been jealous and asked her to go away every time she came around. After a brief meeting with the school social worker, Jackie had agreed not to speak to her unless he wanted to say something nice. I thought it was resolved…until I received the e-mail.

Mia told me that Jackie had become a bully. She wrote that it was so bad that she didn't want to go to school anymore. She implored me to ask Jackie to stay away from her during lunch. I was horrified. I knew that Jackie could be mean. He could throw out comebacks like nobody's business and, in anger, forget his filter. He told it as he saw it. I also knew that he hated her and that it was taking every ounce of restraint that he had to keep it together when he was around her. The hate was deep, too, and it didn't make sense from all the information that I had to go on at the time. After thinking about the situation, I believed her and I felt bad. Jackie could seem like a bully even if he were just reacting out of anger. I told her that I would talk to Jackie and get to the bottom of.

I talked to him the next morning, not accusing him, but trying to get details of what would happen when the three of them were together—the words that were exchanged and the outcome of those words. Nothing really struck me as bully behavior. In most cases, the banter had gone both ways. So I did what I always do when I can't seem to get the whole story, I asked Alexander. Poor Alexander, always in the middle. But he's an honest kid, and I always know that I'll get to the truth in the end. He told me that they were still arguing but that it didn't seem like that big of a deal. I decided that the social worker should step in again, especially since this was causing Mia so much distress. Soon after, Jackie came home one day in complete anger, using every swear word in the book to complain about Mia.

"She called me a name!" he yelled in outrage. "She called me a name, and all I did was go up to Alexander and talk to him."

"Can you tell me everything from the beginning?" I asked, trying to keep it together. I didn't want to accuse him, but I needed to understand what role he had in all of this and explain it to him.

"I am!" he screamed even louder. "That's all that happened! I went up to Alexander and tried to talk to him, and she called me a name!"

"Did you say anything after that?"

"Yes," he replied. "I said, 'Is that the best you can do?'" I had to hold back a smile. That is a really good comeback. "And then she said that I was bullying her."

Hmmm, something wasn't right here.

Surprisingly, later that night, I received another e-mail from Mia asking once again that I keep Jackie away from her and adding the additional request that Jackie should also stay away from Alexander. I e-mailed her back, asking for her view of what had happened that day. She wrote that she had not called Jackie a name and that she was sorry if he thought that she had. Time to ask my Peep. What Alexander told me made me pause and reconsider the events and my eager willingness to believe that Jackie was capable of being a bully. He told me that everything that Jackie had said was the truth. Mia had been jealous that Jackie was talking to him and had been upset that she had been asked to see the social worker. She blamed Jackie for this and called him a name because of it. The whole thing seemed so dumb, so ridiculous. I mean, who cares if someone called you a name, who cares if so and so is jealous and needs to lash out with name calling? Mia's opinions shouldn't mean anything to Jackie. Most kids would just laugh it off, walk away, stay away from her, or tell her to go jump in the lake and be done with it. Even Alexander gave me a sigh of exasperation, thinking that the whole thing had been way overplayed. But the black and white thinker in Jackie's head couldn't rationalize why he was being called a bully when he was doing what he was supposed to do and not talk to her at all. Once I had all of the information, the e-mails made sense. Mia had wanted me to keep Jackie away so that she could hang out with Alexander alone. In a way, I get that. They don't have a lot of time together. But I'm not into exclusion. I went directly into Jackie's room and told him that Alexander told me what happened and that I believed him. I reinforced that he had done the right thing and that Mia was really the one who started it this time. I added, "That was a really good comeback, too," and tried to help him see where Mia might have been coming from, why she had wanted to spend time with Alexander alone. So a situation that should have been crystal clear took me a week to figure out, and that's how it is for us parents of kids with ASD. Getting to the truth is an analytical process that takes time, but it's an important process. Getting to the truth is the only way to teach our kids how to be responsible adults. They just can't learn how the world works unless it's explained to them.

A few months later, after Mia again attempted to include Jackie, they became good friends and still are to this day. She is a sweet girl who was caught in the web of ASD and the misunderstandings that it can create. Alexander helps her understand when Jackie says something inappropriate or seemingly offensive, and she cuts him some slack. Alexander also lets Jackie know when he needs to apologize, and the three of them can hang out and enjoy what the others have to offer. It's a great ending.

CHAPTER THIRTEEN

As middle school progressed, the workload became harder to manage. It wasn't necessarily that the work was too difficult; it was more that the organization of it all became a bigger problem. Jackie had been placed in accelerated math in seventh grade, and he was really excited about that. He had spent the previous summer learning algebra so that he could advance. I'm not sure that his love of math had him focused on advancement; it was more because most of his friends were in advanced classes, and this was just another way to fit in. Once the new concepts were explained to him, he picked up on them quickly, but there were two problems. First, he sometimes found it difficult to concentrate in class, and this led to an inability to do the homework later on. Second, the homework load was heavier. He would open the door of the car at pick-up time and immediate say, "I've got a lot of math homework," in a disgruntled and panicked voice. The minute we got home, he would pull out his iPad and begin the work. Jackie's idea of a lot of homework was fifteen minute's worth. He had a resource class that allowed him an hour every day to stay on top of it all. So even the smallest amount that he had to finish at home caused him stress. Most days, he could get it all done easily, and then he was ready to relax for the rest of the night. Some days, he realized that he didn't understand the math and he would become frustrated. Those nights could explode in anger.

Near the end of the year, Jackie had a lot going on. His weekends were filled with Science Olympiad events and church activities. With the approach of confirmation looming over him, things were piling up. There was a church retreat weekend where he would be going away to an overnight camp for the first time without me. That really stressed him out. He had several major tests the following week, and the math homework was frustrating him. I went into his room when I heard him scream in frustration.

"Is there anything I can help you with?" I asked, knowing that the math was probably too hard for me.

"No," he replied in anger. "I don't understand this math, and I have to get it done today because we have a test tomorrow!" I glanced over his shoulder to the complicated equations illuminated on his tablet.

"Is there someone you can text about it?"

"No!"

"Well, what should we do?" I asked. His eyes met mine, and I thought I saw a fire blazing there, ready to explode. I was right.

"Mom, stop it!" he yelled. "You're making it worse!"

"I'm just trying to help you come up with a plan." I was surprised by how calm I was in the face of the tornado that was coming.

"Stop it!" he screamed. *Here it comes…* "I can't take it! I hate this! It's too much stress! I want everyone to go to hell! I want to die and go to hell! I don't care about confirmation or homework or anything! I just want it to all end. I hate my life!" He threw the iPad, crying now, looking around for someone or something to hit. I was so glad that I had nipped that in the bud years before. I sat there on his bed watching, waiting. I thought about how, five years ago, this scene would have launched me into my own tears, put the fear of God in me, and how I would have just lost it in the agony that I know he feels. But this time, I remained calm because I knew that somehow we'd find a way to work it out. I was just so glad that he was able to tell me what was wrong by using words, even if they were words shouted at the top of his lungs. His sad eyes watched me. They were the eyes of defeat, of a boy who was trying so hard to be strong, but who, in that moment, just couldn't be. He was broken and thought that he couldn't be fixed. I pulled him toward me, and he collapsed in my arms, tears coming faster.

"It's going to be OK," I whispered. "I promise we will work this all out."

"But, Mom," he sobbed. "I have this test tomorrow, and then the overnight on Saturday, and then confirmation stuff on Sunday. I don't have any time for myself, and then I have another test on Monday that I haven't studied for." I hugged him closer and could feel his breathing even out.

"It's not as bad as you think. You'll have time on Sunday afternoon. What's your test on Monday?"

"Life skills," he whispered. We both knew that the last life skills test had been a doozy. It dealt with concepts like empathy and relationship building, things that seemed so abstract to him. Sensing my worry, he added, "It's OK. The test is just on sexually transmitted infections."

Great.

"Here's what we're going to do. E-mail your math teacher. Tell her that you need help understanding some of the problems, and ask if you can come in early tomorrow for a refresher. Then on Sunday afternoon, we'll study for the test and do any other homework, but I'll make sure that you get plenty of breaks. We'll save Saturday afternoon for a movie because I know you'll be tired after the sleepover." He began to calm down, and I watched as he e-mailed his teacher.

"Better?"

"Yeah, but do I have to go on the retreat? I mean, I don't really care about confirmation."

"Yes, it's important, not just for church. This will be a big step for you, doing this without me. You need to be more independent."

"But what if some crazy guy with a knife breaks in and kills us?" He was dead serious.

"That won't happen," I replied firmly.

"It might."

"Is that what you're afraid of?" I asked, wondering where this fear came from.

"Yeah."

"Well, I know that there will be bunk beds. Just make sure you get on a top bunk as far away from the door as possible."

"Mom!"

"You'll be fine," I said with a laugh.

"OK."

The math test went fine, and when he got back from the overnight, he told me that he did get a top bunk, but it happened to be the closest to the door, and he still lived. He didn't eat anything while he was away except for a bar of chocolate at the bonfire, and his toiletry bag wasn't touched. We would work on that. Studying for the life skills test turned out to be disgusting and embarrassing, involving the symptoms and causes for infections like gonorrhea and syphilis. He did fine though. It all worked out. That's the lesson, really. How do we deal with stress—both of us? He freaked out when too much was piled on, but he had been able to tell me why. I didn't freak out, and I was able to listen.

Since then, there have been days when I've found myself overwhelmed by life. I've found myself screaming at the top of my lungs about some seemingly miniscule issue. And Jackie's been there, looking horrified but calm, telling me to relax, and telling me it's not that bad. He's been the one to listen, and that gives me even more hope. Would we be able to forge into the future with this symbiotic kind of relationship? It probably wouldn't always be this way, but at least I knew it could happen. It was a step, anyway.

Autism is hard. It's time consuming and frustrating. But even through all the crap: the people who don't understand, the horrible social situations, and the nights of crying and yelling, I see all of the good. I think about the year when all he wanted for Christmas was a LEGO set and how happy he was when he saw it sitting under the tree. How he watched me put it together because, at nine, his fingers weren't able to fit the pieces together. After three long hours, and with my head ready to explode, I watched him play with the giant LEGO SpongeBob pineapple, and he gave me a smile telling me what a great job I had done. Then, five years later, how all he wanted from Santa was plutonium, yeah that glowing radioactive stuff that's illegal to buy on the open market. I spent weeks scouting for bluish glow in the dark material, test tubes, and even a radio-active-shielded box. I printed off yellow radioactive stickers, and in the end, it had turned out pretty well. On Christmas morning, there it was along with a yellow jumpsuit that would protect him from the rays. Who cared about the rest of us and our soon-to-be mutated cells? Then there was Chernobyl Day when he insisted on having a celebration in remembrance of those who lost their lives in the nuclear explosion. Ordering the giant cookie with Chernobyl written in orange frosting was one of the most embarrassing things I've ever done, but hey, who was I to complain about a special dessert? Or about his quirky interests, his ability to prattle off ten years' worth of NBA facts he had memorized from a book, the latest car stats, or which Hot Wheels cars had been difficult for collectors to find in the past fifty years. All seemingly meaningless but endearing stuff, when I wasn't frustrated that he was wasting his photographic memory. And above all, his amazing, very dry, and sometimes cheeky, sense of humor. He'd launch into "Your Momma" jokes ending on, *Your momma's so fat...*, and I'd interrupt him and say, "You mean P-H phat, the slang word for meaning awesome or good, right?" Then we would spend months turning everything into P-H, trying to turn the negative into positive slang.

"That shirt is ugly, Mom."

"P-H ugly."

"I hate doing homework."

"P-H hate."

"Mom, you're mean."

"P-H mean."

It worked on everything and, inevitably, just made us laugh. Autism made him stay younger longer. It allowed me hugs when other moms were shunned. It gave me, "I miss you," when other moms were getting, "Go away." He eventually caught up, and I did get my turn at, "Mom, you're embarrassing me," but a year or two after his peers.

CHAPTER FOURTEEN

Six Flags Great America is a big part of our summer. The ADA accommodations they provide are really the best I've seen. Disney World, in that regard, was horrible the first time we visited, with very little to offer kids with ASD, but they are changing. At our visit this year, they did their best to personalize our ADA needs and they listened. The main problem for Jackie is sensory overload. The longer we stay in the park, the bigger the fallout later, and for us, that means anger and anxiety. So the faster we can get on rides and get back to the hotel for a sensory break, the better. It's so frustrating when a big park makes you get a comeback time for a certain ride. This means going through the exit and finding the attendant for each ride. They then give you a time to come back to the ride for immediate entry. The comeback time is usually the same amount of time that the wait line is, and usually you can only do this for one ride at a time. It's clear that whoever designed this ADA plan has no idea of what kids on the spectrum are like. Once, at Universal Studios in California, I had one attendant preach to me about how unfair it would be to let Jackie get on the Transformer ride without having to wait. This was the only ride that Jackie wanted to go on, and he was obsessed. I looked the young college kid in the eye and said, "Please don't tell me what's unfair. Is it fair that my son has trouble making friends? Is it fair that we have a conversation about suicide daily? Is it fair that a fun day out can just as easily turn into a crazy anger fest because of too much stimulation? Is it fair that he can't enjoy pizza or a cheeseburger with his friends and doesn't have the ability to understand any of it?" I stood there watching him shuffle his feet uncomfortably and then, in a loud voice so that everyone in line could hear, I said, "I'm sure that if anyone in line were willing to trade brains with my son and give him a typical one, we would be happy to stand in line. Otherwise, try to understand that this is a day that my son has been looking forward to for a year, and I'm not going to let you or autism ruin it for him." He immediately put us on the ride.

We never have these issues at Great America, and because of this, we have been season pass holders for years. Recently, they changed their ADA accommodations so that the system can't be abused. This includes bringing a doctor's note to keep on file. It's a great thing, but on opening day, the ADA line for registration was long—really long. I waited an hour to give them my information, but the wait gave me a chance to look around and people watch. The family behind me had two small children with the father in one of those big scooters, which I've always thought would be fun to drive. Not fun if it's a necessity, though. About halfway through the wait, the young boy, maybe six or seven years old, left the bench he had been sitting on with his older sister and came running over to his mother. He had seen Bugs Bunny all dressed up and waiting to greet the public. The excitement that he felt was palpable, and I smiled at him as he pulled on his mother's shirt, wanting so desperately to tell her. She was annoyed, with either the wait or the fact that her son was tugging on her, and she looked down at him in aggravation.

"Why aren't you listening to my directions?" she asked in a harsh voice. "I told you to sit down on that bench and not move." The boy looked up at his mother and began to explain. He pointed, jumping up and down eagerly in the direction of the big gray bunny.

"I don't want to hear anything you have to say," replied his mother. "You need to go and sit down on the bench like I told you to." I watched as the boy's head dropped and he walked back over to sit with his sister. My heart broke as tears began to slide down his cheeks, his eyes no longer focused on the funny character but on his own shoes. I thought, *Why?* Why would anyone parent that way? Have we as grown-ups forgotten the excitement of youth? Have we decided that our children will do better learning to obey authority rather than having their own voices? When I told Jackie the story, he pointed out that we really didn't know anything about that boy and his family. That boy might have been a real handful, a rebel. I couldn't imagine that, at such a young age, but it got me thinking about respect and how, in our society, we really believe that children don't qualify for it. I think that's a problem.

Jackie had a chess coach who was hardcore. He believed in good posture, clear minds, and quiet. I felt as if every lesson was filled with commands; *sit up, focus, just listen, and don't talk.* It worked for a while. Jackie felt intimidated and wanted to please his coach so he tried to follow the rules. Over time, though, he became so worried about his posture that his focus was on sitting up straight rather than on chess moves so that, inevitably I had to have a conversation with the coach. I asked him to tone it down a notch and explained that Jackie really needed a coach who could just focus on the chess. The coach looked at me and replied, "You know, I really didn't want to say anything, but you really have a big problem."

"OK."

"You talk so much about autism that you're basically allowing Jackie to be autistic. If you would just stop, I really believe that he would get over it." He paused and smiled at me as if he'd just given me the advice that was going to change my life. "Really, just think about it. Maybe a little intimidation is just what he needs."

Wow, for being such a smart man, you're really stupid, I thought. That was the end of that chess coach. I also e-mailed him a ton of information about ASD, along with medical studies and blogs from parents with ASD kids. I hoped he would read everything, but I doubt he did.

⇐⊹⊹⇒

I was really forced into the whole idea of respect and compromise. *Because I said so,* and *just do what I say,* don't work with kids on the spectrum. They need to know the *why* of everything in order to understand and then, hopefully, comply. This is also true in the classroom and had been one of Jackie's issues early on. Helping him is all about words.

"Today at school, my teacher took away my magazine," Jackie cried one Friday afternoon.

"Why did she do that?"

"I don't know." He looked at me questioningly. "I don't think she'll give it back."

"She'll give it back," I replied reassuringly. "Were you looking at it when you were supposed to be doing something else?"

"I don't think so. Kevin was looking at his book, and she didn't take his away."

"Oh."

I met with the teacher the following Monday and asked her what had happened. She said that it had been time to move on to something else and that she had given Jackie several warnings, but he wouldn't put his magazine away, and so the consequence was to take it.

"Did you tell him why he needed to put it away?" I asked a little sheepishly. She glanced at me with a look that clearly told me she was resisting rolling her eyes.

"I think my exact words were, Jackie it's time to put your magazine away." She paused, a little exasperated. "I mean, I think that's clear enough."

"Jackie told me that Kevin was still reading his book. Is that true?"

"Well, yes. Half of the class continues reading and the other half moves on to writing. It's easier to divide up the kids by ability."

"I think that was the problem for Jackie. You have to understand that if he sees a classmate still reading, he thinks that it's OK for him to continue, even if you verbally tell him it's time to move on. He probably wasn't listening to you anyway because he can lose himself in books when he's focused."

"Look," she replied frustrated. "I think that Jackie has the ability to know when it's time to move on and put his magazine away. It just seems like you use a lot of excuses." I felt bad. I *was* using a lot of excuses for him. It did seem like I was always blaming everyone else for the trouble that Jackie got into, but in my mind, there was such a simple way to get everyone on the same page: respect.

"I know it seems that way. I'm really not trying to place blame or make excuses. I'm just trying to show you how he sees things. It's just different from how typical kids see things," I said. "The truth is it's all in the words you use. If you had sat down next to him and said, *I know you're enjoying your magazine, but you're in the group that has to move on to writing now. Once we get through writing there may be more time to read,* he probably would have immediately put the magazine away because then he would have understood why Kevin was allowed to continue reading *his* book."

It was really that simple, but it would mean that his teachers had to take the extra time to voice *the why*. It would mean changing the way they communicated with their classes. It would involve listening to students when they had concerns and finding compromises. Just about the time Jackie entered middle school, our school system made the switch to the SEL program, the program that involved Social Emotional Learning. The SEL program developed by CASLE (Collaborative for Academic, Social, and Emotional Learning) encompasses everything that I was trying to convey to Jackie's teachers at my IEP meetings. That is, a child's emotional welfare directly correlates with learning. From that point forward, teachers had to be trained by social work staff, and they had to learn how to talk differently to their students. Now *all* students would be learning how to form relationship skills, be in touch with emotions, and become self-aware—not just ASD kids. It was years too late for Jackie to benefit from, but it gave me hope for the new batch of kids on the spectrum coming through our school system.

As time went on, I had to take a good look at my advocating and myself. I didn't want to make excuses for Jackie, and I certainly knew that sometimes he could be difficult, even when everything *was* explained to him. Balancing the advocacy line was difficult, but I always remembered his neurologist's words at our first IEP meeting: *anything that will make his life easier we should do, because life will be hard enough for him with ASD.* So I continued to intervene when Jackie felt misunderstood. I continued to explain how to make things easier for him to understand. I fought when I felt that the consequences were way out of line until, finally, in seventh grade Jackie decided he could advocate for himself. The truth is that most teachers appreciated all of this. Out of all his teachers, from second through eighth grades, only a few were difficult to work with. We were very lucky to be in a school system that really cared.

Looking back, the foundation he had was good. We could clash over his wanting two desserts. He would ask for another bowl of ice cream, and I would say no. He would immediately fall into the rage of not getting what he wanted, and I would remember that I shouldn't be reactive. Then I would explain the *why*: if you eat too much ice cream, you might get sick to your stomach and then not be able to sleep. He would object and say that he was still hungry. I would find a compromise. How about a small bowl of peanuts or another slice of bread? Reluctantly, he would choose. That's what respect looks like to me: listening, hearing, talking, and compromising, and I think those skills set him up to be a good advocator.

His teachers would tell me that whenever there was a conflict, Jackie would always come up with an alternative plan, something that would give him a part of what he wanted while still following a classroom rule. Sometimes it works for him, and sometimes it doesn't, but I think the teachers really appreciate his negotiating skills. In the end, we've all heard it before, you really have to pick your battles. Will it kill him if he wants a second bowl of ice cream if it means he'll get it himself? No. That's a step in the right direction toward independence. Is it really so terrible if he chooses a horrible combination of clothes to wear to church? No. He's taking the initiative to pick them out and taking an active role in his self-care. As an ASD parent, I know how important these steps are for Jackie so I let some things go. I give him some control because most of his life is so out of his control.

CHAPTER FIFTEEN

Throughout elementary school and middle school, I waited patiently for Jackie to catch up to his peers, but it never happened. He made progress, grew emotionally, and even became more mature—not as bothered by the differences that he felt. He was still on Planet A, but he had a few good friends joining him there from time to time. It was difficult for me to watch as his peers changed. His friends' interests began to grow, changing as they matured, becoming multifaceted. They would greet me politely, look me in the eye, and tell me all about the newest books they were reading, or introduce me to the video games that were the best. Alexander familiarized me with Five Nights at Freddy's, a game too scary for Jackie at the time, which was not necessarily a bad thing. I begged Jackie to read *The Hunger Games* or *Maze Runner*, but he just stuck with his car magazines. And all the while, his peers were growing up, getting excited about class projects, and filling me in on cool texting lingo and drug issues that they were facing in school. A small part of me was glad that Jackie was so naive, that he didn't care about all of that stuff. He was safe in his own head with his cars. But the bigger part of me wanted him to be aware the same way that his friends were. I worried about the trouble he could get into by not understanding the new maturity level of his peers. As they all entered middle school, his peers began to accept that it was time to leave behind some things, while Jackie was still stuck in second grade.

<hr />

"Hey Mom," Jackie called to me from his bathroom. "I've got a loose tooth!"

"Does it hurt?"

"A little."

"Should I pull it out?"

"I don't know." He looked worried as I took a tissue and pinched it around the wobbly tooth that was hanging on by a thread, and squeezed gently. It popped right out, and I held it up for him to look at. He was thirteen, it was right around Christmastime, and he was excited that the tooth fairy would come and leave him a gift. Of course, all his friends knew that the tooth fairy was a scam and they were also in on Santa and the Easter bunny. But Jackie really believed. I hadn't been able to bring myself to crush those beliefs yet. I was afraid that he would be so disappointed, but I knew that the time was coming.

Jackie wrapped that small bloody tooth in a clean tissue, tucked in under his pillow, and I was nervous. Gone were the days of falling into a deep sleep at eight o'clock. Now it was common for him to wake up from time to time or keep his light on a little later. I just felt like something was about to go wrong. I said goodnight, turned off his nightstand light, and suggested that he get to sleep right away so the tooth fairy could come, and he gave me a big smile. Several hours later, I stood by his bedroom door clutching a dollar bill and a new Hot Wheels car. I eased the door open and saw, with relief, that Jackie was fast asleep. I was scared. I approached the bed and gently slid my hand under his pillow retrieving the wad of tissue and replacing it with the gifts. As I made it back to the door and quietly closed it, I sighed in relief. Then I heard it.

"Mom, is that you?" I pushed open the door and saw him sitting up in bed, his nightstand light turned on.

"What's wrong?" I asked in mock concern.

"Were you just in here?"

I thought fast. "Oh, yeah, I thought I heard something." Jackie reached under his pillow and pulled out the dollar and the car. "Wow, I must have actually heard the tooth fairy!" He stared at me, his sly eyes questioning.

"Mom, what's going on?"

"Nothing. Really. I was just here to check on you." His face fell, and he lay back down on his pillow.

"Mom, tell me the truth." His lip quivered, his eyes filled up, and I wondered if he was upset because he had realized that the tooth fairy wasn't real or because he thought I was lying. I decided to let it all out and expose myself. I perched myself on the edge of his bed.

"OK. I'll tell you, Jackie. I'm the tooth fairy." He looked at me, his eyes wide in shock. I was confused by his reaction. I'm sure he'd heard the rumors in school, other kids dispelling the myths.

"Whoa," he said, a smile edging on the corners of his mouth. "How do you do it?"

"What do you mean?" Now I was really confused. He must know that I just made the switch while he was sleeping.

"I mean, how can you get to all of the houses in the world where someone loses a tooth? There must be hundreds a day! Do you travel while I'm asleep or while I'm at school?" Of course he would take *I'm the tooth fairy* literally! For a second I thought I should roll with it, but he wanted the truth so I corrected him.

"No, I mean I'm the tooth fairy for you, just like other parents are for their kids." His face immediately fell.

"Oh."

"I'm sorry, Jackie, but you wanted to know the truth." He wasted no time with his next question.

"What about Santa?"

"Me."

"The Easter bunny?"

"Me."

"And there really are no leprechauns that live in the forests of Ireland?"

"Well, now that I can't be sure of," I said with a smile. "Are you OK?"

"Yeah. I kind of had my suspicions," he replied. "Thanks for telling me."

It was a rough night but a good one too. He had been ready to know the truth, it had gone well, and that had been my strategy all along: wait until he's ready. With the IEPs, I had always added more accommodations with the idea that, when he's ready, we can get rid of some. When he needed to test separately from his class so that he could remain focused, that's what he did. One day around sixth grade, he told his teacher and the social worker that he didn't want to do that anymore, that he wanted to stay with his classmates, and it worked. When he was ready to try using his locker in eighth grade because he felt comfortable with his schedule and wanted to fit in more with his peers, that's what he did, and there was no more anxiety.

I realized that, even though he might never be at the same emotional and maturity level as his peers, he was changing and that those changes were appropriate for him. That's when I decided to stop waiting for him to catch up. I decided just to celebrate all of the positive steps that he made for himself. I knew that I would have to push a little in the future. There would be a time when he would want to go off to college, and I would have to make sure that he was ready. But I pushed that to the back of my mind for the moment. It was just too much to think about.

The drug issues hit the school seemingly out of nowhere. I had my suspicions well before Jackie hit sixth grade. I had heard rumors that drugs did exist, but I figured that the kids smoking pot out in the back of the school would be the loners, the kids who felt friendless and so spent most of their time with their big brothers. Wow, that was so not the reality of it. Jackie got a DM, direct message, from a friend on Instagram. He talked about buying a vapor device from a kid in the popular group at school. I had no idea what that was, but I was thanking God that I had decided to monitor Jackie's social accounts. You wouldn't believe the information you can get on places like Instagram. Jackie didn't know either, so I went to my main source of shady information, Alexander. He filled me in. A vapor device is designed for aromatherapy or to stop smoking. It can be cigarette shaped or come in the form of a small flask-shaped container. It vaporizes oils and herbs, sending water vapor to your lungs instead of smoke. They're easy to get. Even Amazon carries them and the herb that the kids are vaping is, of course, marijuana.

When Jackie found out what it was all about, he told his friend that he shouldn't do it because it was bad for him. But I remember what it was like back in middle school. I think I would have done anything to be in with the "in crowd," and that was his friend's plan. He wanted to be cool, but unfortunately, being cool involved vaping. I wish that adolescent brains could just bypass all of this crap: alpha groups, survival of the fittest, and the overwhelming need to fit in. The whole thing exploded in his friend's face. Within twelve hours of that Instagram DM, the school was abuzz with the talk of vaping. The under-the-table exchange of money for goods was discovered, and the parties involved were sent to the principal's office. It was a big deal. Jackie's friend was grounded for a month, and blame was thrown around in the form of more Instagram DMs. But the great thing is that Jackie came out of it unscathed. He continued to tell his friend that drugs are bad and that he shouldn't get involved. Jackie could have been a lemming, following the vaping community off the edge of the cliff, but he knew better. I think I have ASD to thank for that. His sensory issues influence what he can and can't do. I'm pretty sure his taste buds couldn't handle whiskey, and when the school teaches about drugs, drinking, and the damage they can do, Jackie takes it as the law. The black and white thinker doesn't see the gray area of peer pressure. If they'd only tell him that swearing causes your ears to fall off, then we'd be in good shape.

CHAPTER SIXTEEN

At Christmas of eighth grade, Jackie decided that he wanted to pick out the tree. It had to be fluffy and tall, really tall. He found a good one at The Home Depot, and we tied it on top of the car and drove it home. Once it was up and decorated, Jackie announced that the tree would be known as Steve Nash, the basketball legend. This didn't surprise me at all, since for the past month everything of importance to Jackie was named Steve Nash. We had the Steve Nash ball that Jackie loved to kick around, the Steve Nash toothbrush, the Steve Nash Star Wars Lightsaber. He had already voiced the idea that Steve Nash was also his spirit animal. It went on and on for months. I figured that it was an appropriate name for the Christmas tree since it stood tall enough to touch the ceiling. But when every sentence began and ended with the words *Steve Nash,* I considered contacting the retired basketball player to ask if he could please change his name.

We've gone through many of these obsessions, and though it can become irritating, it gives me hope for expanding Jackie's interests. We went through Dude Perfect, a group of totally cool guys doing stunts on YouTube, and Jeremy Wade, an amazing extreme fisherman. He would watch the videos, read the books, absorb all the information he could find, and that would be all we could talk about for as long as the fixation continued. It was a needed break from cars, though we always came back to them in the end. But sometimes, the obsessions centered on things that I didn't necessarily want to talk about. The onset of sex ed brought on a whole new load of words and ideas to preoccupy our minds. The seventh grade jargon was the mechanical aspect of it all. *Penis* and *vagina* were words that I heard every ten seconds and that had to be incorporated into just about every sentence. Scrotum, testes, urethra, vulva were all words that became necessities in everyday life. This then launched into inappropriate joking that really made no sense.

"Jackie, can you please put your dirty clothes into the hamper?"

"Oh, I'll put them in, if you know what I mean." He laughed heartily. "Get it? Put it in?"

We'd be in the car with Alexander, and I'd say, "Jackie, please don't touch Alexander. He needs his personal space."

"Oh, I'll give him his personal space, if you know what I mean." He laughed as if he'd just said something shocking.

"What?"

It went on like that for a while until the novelty wore off. I tried to explain to him that most of it really didn't make sense and that the innuendos that did were inappropriate, but he just thought the whole thing was funny. The fun came to an abrupt end in eighth grade and the move from anatomy to sexually transmitted infections, STIs.

Around this time, Jackie was developing acne, something we were continually fighting with various cleansers and mud masks. He would come home from school worried that he had herpes because a zit had developed on his lip. If he felt warm, he was concerned that he was coming down with a fever and that he had developed HIV. He began to worry that I would die or that I would develop some horrific illness. Every day, there was some cause for concern, but it was worse on the days that he had sex ed class.

During all of this, I developed a bad ear condition that went on for months. I felt as if there was something blocking my eustachian tube, and it became so frustrating. It was the first time I had ever been sick for an extended period of time, and at the beginning, I couldn't do as much as I normally could. This only increased Jackie's fear that I would die. We had many talks about how STIs are spread and about the difference between my ear infection and something far worse. My issue was viral and would be better eventually. One night, trying to make a joke out of it, I asked him to look into my ear. He did, but with trepidation.

"Do you see any little face looking back at you? Because I feel like there's someone living in there." He quickly glanced in and then gave me a look of terror.

"What's living in there?" He asked, breathlessly.

"Did you see something?"

"No, but you said there'd be a little face."

I laughed and told him that I was just kidding, that I was trying to show him that I would be fine. I picked the wrong joke to play at the wrong time. From that day forward for the next six months, Jackie would ask me several times a day if something was going to happen to me.

When I would drop him off at school, he'd step out of the car, turn toward me, and say, "Are you going to be all right today? Are you going to be here to pick me up?" I would go for a walk, and he'd ask if I would make it home alive. Just when it was starting to freak me out, the anxiety ended with the final sex ed class. We went back to cars, and I was thankful.

Anxiety plays a big role in most kids on the spectrum. I think a lot of Jackie's anxiety comes from not understanding certain situations and people, as well as from not being understood himself. Sometimes that anxiety can look like he doesn't care or that he's being lazy, but that's usually not the case. Jackie grew up with the same crowd of peers, for the most part. I think that out of everyone who knows him, 90 percent know about his ASD. Many of these kids would not hesitate to include him on the playground or in the lunchroom, but Jackie continuously thinks that he has no friends. The other day, some boys were throwing around a football after church let out. Jackie stood on the sidelines watching. One of the boys threw the ball to Jackie and invited him to come and join the game. Jackie just stood there looking at the group, not comprehending how they could possibly include him; after all, he didn't hang out with them in school. They were in the popular group. I could see the anxiety on his face but also the sadness. It was confusing him, the whole idea that you can have a different set of friends for different events, or that you can still be friends with someone even if they aren't in your group at school. He just tossed the ball back and said, "That's OK."

As I thought about that situation, I could see how his anxiety could look to the other kids like he didn't want to be friends. I could also see other areas where his anxiety could have played a role in other aspects of his life. In class, his anxiety over a schedule change might manifest as willful misbehaving, or even as becoming the class clown. In elementary school, that had been a common event. He would regularly fall on the ground and act silly. At the time, we all thought he was just trying to fit in somehow, and that humor might be his thing, but looking back, I see that it was most likely his way of handling his anxiety. He needed a way to release that energy, especially in the face of not being able to control most of what happened in his day. I also see a real correlation with anxiety and anger. There have been two or three peers, throughout the years, with whom Jackie has clashed. I was horrified the first time that he came to me and told me that he wished one of these peers were dead. He would come up with scenarios of how to make them leave the country or get injured so that they couldn't come back to school. The anger that he felt was so intense that he would go on rants about how deeply he hated this person or how he couldn't go back to school because of this person. It was concerning. But as I thought about the situations, I began to make the connection. There is sometimes a thin line between hate and hurt, and the hurt and anxiety that Jackie felt on a daily basis were snowballing into anger. All of this anger really stemmed from constantly feeling misunderstood, and with this small handful of peers, there was a deep misunderstanding of who Jackie was.

I think that one of the hardest things about being a parent of an ASD kid is the never-ending rollercoaster ride. These awful peer situations were draining, not only in dealing with Jackie's anger and hurt feelings but also in trying to understand where the other kid was coming from. In the end, all these hate issues were resolved. After working with the school social worker and through the advancement of time, Jackie realized that these kids weren't so bad, and that, in turn, helped these kids accept Jackie. Sometimes the resolution came in a few months, other times it took a year, but it all ended well. And there I'd be, a little more banged up and a lot more tired, wondering why we couldn't have just sorted the whole thing out sooner. The truth is that if we are ever going to see life through their eyes, we have to take the journey with our kids. We can't assume that their behaviors are ever what they seem. Sometimes they are, but most of the time, it's us typical folks who aren't getting the big picture, and the spectrum kid can't understand why. Honestly, having a spectrum child is an opportunity to see the world in a completely new way, a deeper way, and I feel very lucky to have that opportunity…most days.

CHAPTER SEVENTEEN

As Jackie turned thirteen, puberty came at me like a lion tearing through the savanna, his eyes fixed on me, the unsuspecting, innocent gazelle. I got the usual stuff: the eye rolling, the secrecy, and the gasps of exasperation over things that I couldn't possible understand, but I also got more anger. Jackie became increasingly more difficult to talk to, which made it hard to get to the heart of any problem. He wanted to lock himself in his room, play video games. or look at car magazines. He wanted to be alone. I found myself sitting on my bed at the end of each night thinking, *yeah, one of us needs to be medicated.*

It seemed to happen overnight. One day he was telling me everything, giving me way too much information, and the next, his lips were sealed. It went from the three of us—Jackie, Alexander and I—hanging out to Jackie's insistence that I should back off. I oftentimes found myself in the movie theater in the fifth row alone while the boys headed to the top row. Some of the changes were good. I was glad that he was depending less on his mother. It was natural and made me feel like he would do OK with some independence. He was ready. I was ready. I was happy that he wanted to do more on his own, and this included most of his homework. I stopped worrying when I got a Power School ping on my iPad telling me that his algebra grade had gone down to a B. He began to take care of things like this by talking to his teachers or following up on assignments that he might have forgotten about. So puberty wasn't all bad, but the bad sure outweighed the good. The screaming fits happened daily, and his self-image and self-esteem seemed to take a spiraling spill into the dark abyss of loathing. There seemed to be nothing I could say to make him believe that, yes, he's a good-looking boy, and no, not everyone has a girlfriend in middle school. The desire to fit in was overwhelming, and I began to wonder what had happened to all the work we had done toward helping him accept himself. Where was the celebration of Jackie? I thought we had been on the same page that being different is good. All of the book signings, the teacher chats, the chess trophies, and the praise of his steel-trap mind, all flushed down the toilet in a swirl of social misfit-ism. I would say, "You know, none of your school mates have published a book."

"No one cares, Mom."

"OK, but how many have over thirty chess trophies?"

"No one cares, Mom."

"Well, what about your perfect GPA or National Honor Society?"

"No one cares, Mom."

The truth is that I really didn't know how I would get through four years of high school if this continued. I began to think about issues like teen suicide, cutting, and self-medicating with drugs or alcohol—all things for which I would have to keep an eye open. The new secrecy left me wondering how safe he really was. Would he come to me if confronted with the prospect of drugs? My answer came sooner that I thought it would.

Jackie's circle of friends is small but loyal. The group has been together for years, and I have spent time with them, getting to know what they're into and getting the scoop on what's cool these days. But one of the boys in the group struggles. He's had serious issues at home and at school, trying to fit in, make, and keep friendships. His life hasn't been easy, and of course, Jackie and I can relate to that. I've always tried to help him whenever I could, but it's hard to focus on someone else when your own child has become a raging ball of hormones. One night, Jackie was logged into his Instagram account, and I saw that he was watching a video. I nonchalantly peeked over his shoulder, and he immediately tried to hide it.

"Mom, this is private!" Praying that he wasn't looking at videos of half-naked women or worse, I asked him what the big deal was.

"You know, I follow the same people that you do so I can probably go into my own account and see it," I said, as if I didn't care at all. He seemed to think this was true so he turned the iPad toward me. There, in front of me, I saw his friend's face, apparently in a video he had made and posted in a DM to a small group. He was giving a demonstration on how to smoke. It was strange seeing a kid that I had known since he was a little boy, puffing away, with a halo of smoke encircling his head. My mind went to those memories: the summer play that I directed, giving him a lead role, the trips to fun places, the autism walks for charity. I watched the screen as smoke blew all around him, hoping that the cigarettes contained tobacco and nothing more. I was dumbfounded, shocked, and worried.

"You haven't smoked, have you?" I asked, ungluing my eyes from the video.

"Right, Mom, really? You think I'm that stupid?" No, I didn't, and in that moment, I thanked the sensory integration disorder gods. There would be no way that Jackie could ever think of smoking, or drinking for that matter.

"We have to tell someone," I said. "This could lead to something worse, like smoking pot."

"Oh, I'm pretty sure he's already done that," Jackie replied with certainty. *Lord, first the vaping, and now smoking, and maybe pot!* I thought.

"We should tell his parents," I said. "Maybe not about the pot, but definitely about the smoking."

Jackie sat quietly for a moment, watching the thirty-second video play over and over again, and then replied, "We can't tell anyone."

"Why?" I retorted. "Jackie, he could get into some really bad stuff. Smoking is like a bridge to drugs, especially at your age. Plus, we don't want him to get sick."

"I tell him every day how bad it is. He's never going to stop. There's nothing we can do." There was something more to this story. I felt it.

"Tell me what's going on," I said sternly.

"Nothing."

"Tell me!"

"Nothing, Mom!"

"You know that either way, I'll find out. I have my sources." He glared at me and huffed something under his breath that sounded suspiciously like a swear.

"Fine...he said that if I tell anyone, he has a secret on me that he will tell."

"Does he?"

"Yes, but it isn't about smoking or drugs or anything like that." When I suggested that it was about a girl, he nodded. *Wow, this was big-time, blackmail!* I needed some time to think about the situation. Was I overreacting? I mean, it's not as if the kid was smoking a crack pipe. People smoked, maybe even his parents smoked. My decision came down to two factors. First, if this had been Jackie smoking, would I want to know? Yes. And second, I knew that the suggestion of blackmail was hanging over Jackie's head, causing him extra anxiety. I could see it in him: the fear and the confusion. Here was his friend whom he wanted to help, but he couldn't. It's a situation that I'm sure many kids have found themselves in, weighing the risk over the reward and thinking that the risk was way too great. But for Jackie, the confusion was in the idea of his friendship. A friend doesn't do things to hurt you intentionally, yet this friend threatened to do just that. Was he really his friend? I asked him why he still wanted to hang out with a boy who would do that to him, and he replied, "He doesn't have anyone to sit with during lunch, and I feel bad for him.

I know how that feels." I was happy that Jackie could feel empathy in this way and relate his own experiences to others who may be going through the same thing. I didn't want to discourage that, but being blackmailed was just too much for me. That was the bigger problem. I asked Jackie how he would feel if I talked to the school social worker about the situation, and he thought it was a good idea. So that's what I did. In that setting, Jackie voiced his concerns about his friend's smoking and about how bad he felt about being blackmailed. His friend wasn't mad at him, for the most part. I'm sure there were consequences for him at home, but I had to talk to him about the blackmail issue. I also wanted him to know that I wasn't upset with him, that I understood that middle school wasn't easy and that we sometimes make bad choices. As for Jackie, a little secrecy is OK. But if it involves sex, drugs, or blackmail, he needs to tell someone even if it means getting a friend busted. It's better to be busted in middle school when there's time to change your wicked ways, than ending up in juvy on a drug conviction.

It's harder for kids with ASD to navigate these waters. They have difficulty understanding basic relationships. When Jackie had his first crush in fourth grade, he stalked her. He would follow her around the playground or sit too close on the rug during reading time. He would become infatuated with one girl, and that would last the whole year until he had some time away during the summer. Years later, the girl told me that Jackie had really creeped her out at first, but that once she got to know him and know about his autism, she was fine with it. Jackie's not a stalker anymore, but I can see shadows of it in his relationships now. He can be possessive and easily hurt by jealousy. He's also loyal to a fault, which is another reason that he didn't say anything about the smoking. I pray that he never gets caught up with the wrong group as he enters college in a few years. He is the kind of guy who will follow happily if you're just nice to him. I just hope that the nice kids are the safe ones.

Puberty is pretty much the same in an ASD kid as in typical kids, with a few exceptions. When you stop to think about all the changes that teens' bodies go through—knowing how difficult change is in the first place—it's not surprising that anger increases during this time. One of the best things that we did was talk constantly about why the anger might exist. I wanted Jackie to know that I didn't think it was necessarily his fault when he was so out of control that I thought he would go crazy but that the anger had to be directed somewhere, not just at me. Having strategies are very important. Most of the time, listening to music or having time alone was all it took. It's such a big accomplishment when Jackie can redirect himself, and that's starting to happen. After a hard day at school, when I see that anger is at the surface, I want to get to the heart of it immediately. But Jackie just looks at me and tells me he needs some time alone when we get home, and I'm good with that. We can address issues after he has time to decompress.

Now that he has a real interest in girls, and knowing that he has been a stalker in the past, we have begun the process of trying to understand certain cues that a girl might give him to tell him that she's interested, or not. ASD kids can have big trouble understanding friendly body gestures or even facial expressions. They don't necessarily understand that if someone is standing in front of you with their arms crossed and looking away that it might mean they really don't want to talk to you.

"Is she giving you the hair flip when you talk to her, Jackie?"

"No."

"Is she leaning in while talking to you?"

"No, she doesn't really talk to me."

"Does she laugh at your jokes?"

"Well, yeah, but everyone does."

"OK, but is she running away screaming if you come too close?"

"No."

"Good, I think your best bet is to put her in the friend category."

I try to encourage him to put all the girls that he likes into the friend category. The best relationships always start with a good-friend foundation. Along with this new social game come more mood fluctuations. Sometimes it's difficult to tell if these mood changes fall into the pit of real depression or if they are just made more extreme because of ASD. Depression can be a real problem. Jackie felt down a lot with feelings of inadequacy. Along with wanting to be alone so often, I became nervous. But, though his moods are extreme, I haven't noticed any changes that really contrast with his normal behaviors. It's just more intense. I do keep my eyes open, though. Depression can be marked by low self-esteem, withdrawal, a change in eating and sleeping patterns, increased agitation, and extreme lethargy, so much so that it contrasts with what is normal for a given child. Good to know.

Puberty is also a time that involves certain social expectations: Where do I belong on the social ladder? How have I changed physically compared to my peers? And how do I fit in? Just when Jackie thought he had the whole game figured out, he entered puberty, and it messed him up. The drug issues, the girl issues, the friend issues, and the uncontrollable changes all make for a confusing time of life.

CHAPTER EIGHTEEN

Over all, middle school had its ups and downs for Jackie. It was a time of real growth. He went from being completely unsure of himself to finding a balance between wanting to fit in and liking the differences that he brought to the table. By the time eighth grade rolled around and I was wondering where the time had gone, his social game was improving. He was happy with his crew, even if I questioned a few of them. He was learning how to be a good friend, wanting to help those peers who were moving in the wrong direction, and taking some criticism while standing up for himself whenever he recognized injustice. He was getting better at making choices for himself and really beginning the process of speaking up in school and being his own advocate. There were still a few touchy moments, and the one thing that he still struggled with was the anger. He could be explosive, reactive, and unhearing. On really bad days, days when I knew he was tired, this anger could escalate. I worried where this would take him in the future.

One exceptionally hot afternoon, Jackie and Alexander decided to hang out at the house. Jackie had just gotten a new computer, something to get him ready for high school, and he wanted Alexander to help him set some things up. Knowing that Alexander is a tech guy, I was glad that Jackie had taken the initiative to ask him for help. They spent time downloading Chrome as a browser and figuring out what other necessities were needed. Then it was time to find the games that Jackie liked and get them loaded on. This process became a little more complicated, and as I sat in my room reading, I heard a loud shout and a bang. Suddenly Jackie appeared in the hallway, stomping around, throwing out profanities, while Alexander sat calmly at the computer. I gave Alexander a questioning glance, and he shrugged as if he had no idea what had set Jackie off.

"What's wrong?" I asked Jackie as he huffed around, looking as if he were ready to punch a hole in the wall.

"I hate that computer!" he shouted. "I hate our cheap Internet! I hate that you can't buy better stuff! This is all your fault!"

"What happened?" I asked again, trying to keep my composure. The calmness in my voice must have sent Jackie over the edge because he ran downstairs, away from the offending computer.

"Honestly," Alexander said, as we heard more shouting and bangs from below us. Jackie was kicking a rubber ball all around the house in a fit of anger. "He's just upset because for some reason the website for his video game won't let him create a membership." I raised my eyebrows in surprise as Alexander gave me another shrug. Either the ball had been damaged beyond repair, or Jackie had calmed down enough to stop kicking it, and I heard his feet padding up the carpeted stairs. He'd decided to return to the scene of the crime.

"Can you fix it, Mom?" he asked.

"I don't think so, not right now." The anger began to bloom again on his face, and Alexander turned to him.

"Jackie, this is nothing. When you're dealing with computers, this stuff happens all the time, and usually it's worse than trying to join a video club."

"But you did it on your iPad, and I should be able to do it, too."

"Look," I added. "We can try to figure it out later, but when stuff like this happens, it's better to just walk away. Maybe the computer needs to reboot— and maybe you do, too."

"Yeah," said Alexander. "You have to have patience when it comes to computers. Believe me; you'll see this kind of stuff a lot."

The anger was over; ending like it always does, quickly. He is like a stick of dynamite. Once the fuse is lit, there is a big explosion, but after the dust settles, it's over. I asked Alexander if Jackie's anger scares him, if he's worried that he'll get caught in the explosion, but he said no. He'd seen it so many times before that he's used to it and knows that Jackie gets over stuff quickly. But I'm not sure others would see it that way. After Alexander went home, I sat Jackie down to talk about what had happened.

"You know, Jackie, sometimes your anger can be scary. You kick that ball around downstairs, and all I can think is what if you didn't have a ball?" He was sad, not to mention tired. The anger takes a lot out of him. He looked at me, pleading with me,

"I feel like I can't control it at all, and I'm really afraid." I wasn't expecting that. All this time, I'd thought he couldn't see his actions as I could. I had no idea that, in those moments when that poor ball was being smacked across the house or when his overused punch pillow had taken the brunt of it all, he had been afraid of himself and of what he felt. He might even have been afraid of what he might do.

"You have to help me, Mom. I don't know what to do or how to make it better." The truth was that I didn't know what to do, either. We had developed techniques like the punch pillow or taking some time out in a safe place, but now we were facing how to deal with this out in the real world. I did the only thing that I could think of and brought the issue to his therapist. Together they spent time developing new, real-world techniques, such as breathing exercises and visualization, and things calmed down for a while, but it's a work in progress.

⟞⟢ ⟣⟝

One glimpse into how the anger exercises were working happened during the summer before high school. I had signed Jackie up for a three-week organizational class, and Alexander had agreed to take it also so that it wouldn't seem too bad. They had to wake up early and be at the high school by eight o'clock. It was a good opportunity to get them ready for the schedule they would have in the coming fall. Jackie complained the entire first week, frustrated that he had to climb out of bed at dawn and sickened by the occasional homework. Every other day, he would tell me how mean the teacher was, and I just put those complaints on the pile, knowing that soon the whole thing would be over. In the final week, trying to get to an appointment on time, I dropped them off in a hurry, and my phone began to ring. It was Jackie. In a calm voice, he asked me to turn around and come back to pick him up. I tried to get more information, but it was clear that he was anxious to get off the phone. I did get bits and pieces of the scene, including a threatening teacher and kids making fun of him. I was determined to head back, defuse the situation, and insist that he go back to class. Jackie had had situations like this so many times—a missed social cue or an unrealistic idea of what was going on around him. In school, he would ask to go to the social worker, and together, they would walk through the problem with great results. But here at summer school, there was no social worker to talk to, and Jackie had gone to the next best person: me.

I arrived back at the school ready to have that *get it together* conversation, and as I approached the classroom and peered inside, the teacher glanced my way with a horrified look on his face.

"I'm sorry, Mr. Johnson. I had a phone call from Jackie, and he seemed upset about something so I just need to have a conversation with him and get it sorted out in his mind." Mr. Johnson was an older man, stocky with white hair and a kind face, kind of a grandfather type at first glance. In a flash, upon hearing my request, that kind face turned to anger.

"Jackie was upset because I said no to him," he retorted coolly. "We have a special chair in the classroom, and he wanted to sit in it. He began arguing with another boy about it, and so I said that no one could sit in it." I could tell what his mind was thinking because it was written all over his face. Spoiled child didn't get his way so now he's called Mommy to come and save him. But I knew that if that was the story, then Jackie would have to accept it and move on, and I was willing to help him do that.

"Oh, OK," I replied. "Then I'll just need to have a conversation with Jackie to make sure that he understands." Mr. Johnson looked long at me, seemingly unwilling to let that conversation take place. I noticed that he was visibly shaking from anger, and I just couldn't understand why. What was the big deal? He knew that Jackie had autism and that he had an IEP so I couldn't understand the anger. Hesitantly, he leaned into the classroom and called for Jackie. As Jackie came to stand in the hallway, I waited for the teacher to leave, but that never happened. Instead, Mr. Johnson's bomb went off.

"Jackie, I am very angry. When I say no, I mean no, and that is not a reason for you to call your mother. You're fourteen years old. You're going into high school, and this kind of thing won't fly there. You should be ashamed of yourself." There was more and worse. It was loud and full of rage, and Jackie stood with his back against the wall crying silently. I took a deep breath, not able to look at Mr. Johnson. I waited for it to be over, for him to get it out so that I could try to have a calm conversation. All I wanted to do was take Jackie by the arm and run. I wanted to find another school, maybe in another state or country, anywhere where people were nice and understanding, but I waited. He stopped abruptly, and I glanced up. Jackie looked back at me imploringly.

"Mr. Johnson," I replied softly. "I have to say that I am really disturbed by your tone."

"Well, I'm very angry."

"Yes, I can see that, but you have to understand that Jackie had no other recourse than to call me. Usually he has a social worker that he can talk to when he doesn't understand something with a teacher or a peer. He doesn't have that here so he contacted the only other adult that he knew: me."

"Well, I told him that he could go to the office. They have counselors there." Jackie's face was red, and he looked completely confused.

"The truth is, Mr. Johnson, I'm having a difficult time understanding your anger, and I feel uncomfortable letting Jackie come back to class." I turned to Jackie. "Let's go and see if we can find a social worker to talk to, and maybe we can resolve this."

We did meet with a social worker, and Jackie refused to go back to the class at first. I felt as if Mr. Johnson's behavior bordered on abusive for any child, but I could also see his side of the situation. High school kids don't call home when dealing with problems. Jackie painted a picture of an even more abusive and threatening teacher, saying that it had been going on for a while and that this had been the last straw. I then asked him what his side of the story was.

"I wanted to sit in the special chair, and so did another boy. When we started to argue about it, Mr. Johnson told us that no one could sit in it. I was trying to explain to him that I won't be in class tomorrow because of my doctor's appointment and that maybe I could use it today and the other boy could use it tomorrow, but he said he didn't care."

"So were you mad about the chair or that he wouldn't listen?"

"I just wanted him to listen, and when he said that he didn't care, that really hurt, and that's when I got upset and called you. I didn't feel safe, and I wasn't sure that I could control my anger." That was a positive step. He wanted to remove himself from a potentially explosive situation before the anger he felt got the best of him. And looking at him then, he was calm. I could see him using breathing exercises, shaking his hands, and trying to get his heart rate down, and it was working. Jackie did go back to class, and I did have another conversation with Mr. Johnson. The better conversation came between the social worker and the teacher. I found out later from Alexander that Mr. Johnson had threatened to send Jackie to the dean's office when he tried to explain himself and that there had been threats throughout the few weeks of class. But I was happy for the experience. I was happy to see that Jackie was learning how to manage his feelings better. Unfortunately, along with the happiness came complete trepidation as I considered the idea that all high school teachers might be like Mr. Johnson.

On the last day of summer school, I met again with Mr. Johnson, and I could see a change. He offered to take Jackie and Alexander on a private tour of their new school, showing them where their classes would be. He was patient, answering Jackie's questions, even the ones that he asked repeatedly. He apologized for not understanding Jackie's issues and for not listening to him. In the end, Jackie reached out his hand and thanked Mr. Johnson, telling him that he wished he could keep him with him during the school year. Mr. Johnson smiled and showed him where his office was, just in case he needed him. And my trepidation dissipated. If the teachers were willing to learn, that's all I could ask for.

CHAPTER NINETEEN

Puberty should be illegal. I wondered how it would all go down with Jackie, hoping for the best, worrying what the worst would look like. It was tough, but as we entered the realm of high school, things began to calm down. The swearing was still an issue, and the complete disregard for all things appropriate continued, but I could see that Jackie was slowly growing up. My mind began to switch from bullying matters and immediate social issues to looking ahead and finding more ways for Jackie to be self-sufficient. This switch had been triggered by our summer trip to Minneapolis and the Mall of America.

Jackie and Alexander were getting to the point where they could share their own hotel room, giving me the night off, even though I was usually situated next door. The first few times this setup came into play, Jackie made the decision to stay up all night, but after several conversations, he promised to turn the lights off at nine o'clock. Our first night in Minneapolis gave him the opportunity to prove the weight of his promise, and I wasn't disappointed. I wandered next door around eight in the morning, and Alexander assured me that Jackie had been asleep early. Jackie seemed proud and blurted out, "See? I did what you wanted. We turned the light out at nine after Alexander got my milk for me, and read me a bedtime story, and tucked me in."

"*And* charged your iPad and phone *and* put your clothes away *and* put your thermos in the fridge," Alexander chimed in.

Whoa, reality check! I could see the boys in my mind's eye, clear as day; sharing an apartment in college, Alexander becoming me, willing to take care of Jackie, doing the things that Jackie should be doing for himself, and Jackie, taking full advantage of it. And I knew how it all looked from the outside: a kid with a misplaced sense of entitlement—a kid who was spoiled and unwilling to take care of himself. If I'm honest, there was probably a little bit of truth to that, but I also knew that it was about something bigger. Jackie associated caregiving as love. It was almost as if he was afraid to do things on his own because he thought that he would be taking something away from me and, that by showing independence, he would be distancing himself from me. When Alexander showed him this kind of care, it was confirmation that Alexander really loved him and that Alexander would be there for him. But even knowing the deeper origins, things had to change. I knew that we would have to take it slow. After talking to his therapist, we both agreed that the best way to deal with this was to let Jackie have some input, maybe coming up with the responsibilities that he felt that he might need to learn.

"Hey, Jackie, I was thinking that it might be good for you to learn some household things. Maybe I could show you how to do laundry, or maybe from now on you could get your own milk." He looked at me questioningly. I continued, "You know, in a few years you're going to have to do this stuff for yourself." He yawned.

"You know, Mom, I really don't want to learn anything that requires work. I'm basically a lazy person and, anyway, I have Alexander for all of that stuff." *It's worse than I thought.*

I knew deep down that Jackie was not a lazy person. I had seen him study hard to win a chess tournament. I knew how much time went into schoolwork.

He had even served me a glass of water in bed with the comment that he was sorry that he didn't know how to make coffee. I had seen his drive begin the process to become a Hot Wheels designer and his wish to intern in Germany at a car manufacturer. I also knew that a lot of what comes out of his mouth is said for shock value or because he thinks he's being funny. Many times, ASD kids are followers. Jackie will copy behaviors or words that other friends have said as he tries to fit in. Alexander and I are always correcting him with this, reminding him that not everyone is a reliable source to mirror. The next day, I showed him how to do laundry and then made him do it by himself, but the first real test came a few days later.

"Mom, I'm hungry. Could you make my lunch?"

"I'm sorry, Jackie, but I have an appointment, and I'm already late. I'll be back in an hour, but you know where everything is so if you're that hungry you can get it yourself." I get a scowl as I rush out the door. I got home an hour later and there he was, sitting in bed, an open jar of peanut butter with a large spoon thrust in the middle, a loaf of bread, and a canister of Pringles. No plate, no napkin, and no milk, but I thought, *Hey, if this is how it goes down in college, at least he'll be eating.* Getting his own milk came next and then charging his own electronic devices. Finally, there came a day when he wanted to stay up later at night. I told him that we could try to push his bedtime back half an hour, but with this new independence would also come responsibility. No more telling him to brush his teeth, no more tucking him in, helping him clean off his bed, or making sure that his computer was turned off. Now all of these responsibilities would be his. He would have to get up in the morning without complaint, and if he felt tired, he would have to make the decision to turn off the light earlier next time. He told me he was ready, and just like when he was ready to use the school locker in eighth grade, he was, and it worked.

There's still a long way to go, but I can see that as he becomes more self-sufficient he also becomes a little more mature. I'm still so worried about the future. I lose sleep over the thoughts and worries about what will happen to Jackie. I feel as if I've aged fifty years in the space of a decade, and I'm so tired. But at least I know that he'll eat.

Along with my worries that Jackie will not be able to take care of himself physically, I also worry that he will be taken advantage of by his peers. The follower instinct kicks in, especially when someone is nice to him. He will follow a friend off a cliff, defend bad behavior, and not always see when he's being used.

He's an easy target. While on our Minnesota trip, that was tested as we entered the glorious dominion of the video arcade. Jackie loves the ball drop games, and he's a master. He can stand at the glowing column and calculate the exact moment to drop the ball into the jackpot hole. It's amazing to watch and usually attracts groupies. This day was no different.

"Jackpot!" Ten minutes later, "Jackpot!" And on and on. He was racking up the tickets, as Alexander and I watched from a distance. We noticed a younger boy hanging out with Jackie, watching, and cheering him on. He was alone with no parents in sight and apparently no game card. At one point, Alexander came up to me and whispered, "That kid just asked me if I would get him a prize from the redemption center." A part of me felt bad, and I thought that maybe I should just get the kid a game card, but I wasn't sure if his parents even wanted him in the arcade at all.

"What did you say?" I asked.

"I just said, 'I don't think so.'" We watched as the boy continued to hang with Jackie. "That kid seems shady," continued Alexander. "I wouldn't be surprised if he asks Jackie for something." We walked over then so that I could get a better feel for the situation.

"Hey," said the kid, glancing up to see me. "I have an idea."

"Oh really, what?"

"Why don't you guys give me your cards, and I'll go and find out how many tickets you have." I turned to Alexander, and we gave each other a knowing look.

"No. That's OK," I replied. "It really doesn't matter."

"OK, maybe if you have enough credits left you could let me play a game," he continued, turning to Jackie.

"Maybe." As Jackie finished the ball drop machine and walked over to the car racing booths, he sat down next to the boy.

"Here, kid, have at it," he said as he swiped his card so that the boy could race with him. I'm torn. How great that he wanted to make someone else happy. It's hard for him to think of others, especially when it means giving up money or the number of games that he can play, so I felt good about that. But as I looked again to Alexander, I knew that this could get bad. What would happen if he were away at college and some deviant moocher decided to be nice to him and then got him to buy food, drugs, or alcohol? What if he ended up in a scary place and didn't know how to say no or was worried that he'd lose a friend if he did say no? What if he couldn't always tell right from wrong in those situations?

The kid continued to follow us around, and Jackie bought him a few more games, but when the kid kept asking, he finally turned to him and said, "I have to keep playing, too. I've won nine jackpots, and I can't end on a nine. So after I win another jackpot, if there's any credits left, we'll see." That's good. However, as we headed to the redemption counter, I got worried again. I knew he had a lot of tickets. The kid started talking about the stuff he wanted. First, it was the small stuff, and Jackie got it for him. That surprised me, and I was glad that he was giving to someone he really doesn't even know. Then the kid started talking about the big prizes, and Jackie again turned to him and said that if there was anything left after Alexander and he were done shopping, he could have it. And there were tickets left, and the kid picked out some candy and a fake mustache and seemed happy. I was proud of Jackie, but Alexander and I both wondered how much he really understood. As we walked back to our rooms, our arms loaded with prizes, Jackie says, "Wow, that kid was good."

"What do you mean?" I asked.

"He was a major salesman, really shady. He was working me like a master."

Alexander and I agreed.

"I'm pretty sure he's done this before," Alexander added.

"I'm just glad you didn't fall for it," I said.

"Yeah, right, like I didn't see it coming a mile away."

"Well, I thought it was nice that you got him some prizes."

"I thought I'd throw the kid a bone."

Yes, I'm still worried. College isn't a video arcade, and college students are a lot smarter than a nine-year-old kid is, but it showed me that maybe Jackie is more in tune than I thought he was. Maybe.

It's hard to be a parent, any parent. It's hard to know when to push your kids or protect them. My most difficult struggle has always been letting Jackie go, letting him get his own bumps and bruises from the world. But now, after years of helping him understand who he is and fighting to help others understand who he is, I find myself frustrated and exhausted. It feels like the struggle never ends. It feels like the autism never gets better or easier, not that I thought it would go away. Part of me thought it might get hidden, that the issues might *seem* better. Certainly, things have changed, but dealing with ASD is like looking through a kaleidoscope. As you turn it, the colors switch, change, and slide into different places, but you can never really make out what they are trying to form. You can never get a real end picture that makes sense. It's depressing after a while, you get sick of trying to make sense of it, and you want to just put the stupid kaleidoscope away and pretend as if it doesn't exist. But it does, you know it's there and you have to keep looking because it's not just about you.

CHAPTER TWENTY

I pulled out some DVDs the other day. They were full of home videos, moving pictures of Jackie's first Christmas, trips to Florida, and his first steps. I wanted to look back and see his childhood through educated eyes, eyes that now know autism. As I watched him at ten months, he was growing fine—no red flags, nothing to worry about. Then around his first Thanksgiving, his first birthday, and Christmas, I noticed something. Through all of it, he rarely showed any emotion, and that's what I remember: no crying and no problems. Looking at it now, I realize that he was in his own head even then. There's one moment where I called his name repeatedly, but he wouldn't look away from his hands. Another time, we were at the zoo. I pointed out the penguins and the emus, and he just looked at me as if he was not interested at all. Throughout all of the twos and threes, he had the same expression on his face, that of disinterest, nonemotional. But he was my first child, and back then, there was nothing to compare him to, so I missed those signals. Spectrum disorders are like that, vague at first.

I looked back, wondering, *If I had known, would I have done anything differently?* The answer is, yeah, probably. But as parents, we all make some mistakes, and in the end, I know that I did the best that I could. Today, Jackie is aware of his ASD. He can talk openly about it and tries to understand how others might see him. It's kind of like being born blind and someone asking you what you think green looks like. You have a perception of that color, but it certainly wouldn't be how the seeing world views it. And as hard as I try to understand Planet A, I know that I never will understand all of its secrets. I'll never be there, in Jackie's mind, seeing the world as he does. We talk about it. We talk and talk and talk until it seems as if I'm almost there and he's almost here, and that's what I want to share—the place of almost knowing. From Jackie's point of view, he just wants to be understood. He just wants other kids with ASD to know that's it's OK to be different.

Looking back, I know that I wouldn't change a minute of what we've gone through. Every child has struggles, bumps in the road, and feelings of inadequacy. All parents wonder if they're doing it right, if the decisions they make for their children are the right ones. Jackie, and maybe autism, too, has done so much for me. Before Jackie, I was never a patient person, but now I have to be. I was never in tune with that deep part of the human experience that really makes us who we are, but now I have become introspective with the ability to relate to a bigger population of people. I am slower to judge a situation, and I have found that love and kindness go so much further than anger and frustration. There seems to be so much to look forward to. Jackie will go on to college at some point or in some form. He may always struggle with relationships, but I'm hopeful that as he matures, he'll be able to navigate that part of his life better. I have seen growth—slow growth—but growth all the same. This is how I look at life now, a progression and a glass half full. As parents, we should see the beauty in our children and show it to them, building on their strengths and making them see how capable they are, even when we question it. As my mother often told me whenever I felt frustrated, "No one ever said that life would be easy." Life isn't easy, but in our house, it sure is extraordinary.

The world around us is changing, too. In so many parts of the world, autism is becoming a common word. Universities, both in the States and around the world, offer many accommodations for kids with neurological differences. These can include audiobooks for textbooks, study partners, and people to help students with ASD with organizational skills. There are social workers, advisers, and student mentors as well. I have also seen a growth in inclusion programs in the workplace for adults with autism. There are companies in the United States that hire only adults on the spectrum, providing them with an environment that works for their brains. Companies have discovered the power of concentration in the autistic brain, especially when it comes to computer work. There is more than hope for our ASD kids; there are viable possibilities. Even if your child is not as high functioning as Jackie is, the awareness that is being created in society, as a whole, will lend itself to opportunities. Our local supermarket has a young adult with ASD on staff to be your personal shopper. Another young man I know is a dog walker. In the years to come, there will be more awareness, and with it, a better understanding of our special kids and all they can contribute.

⊨⊢ ⊣⊨

The Interview
Jackie

1. **What are some things that hurt your feelings?**
   Having to go to school at all. I don't like when
   people call me annoying. I mean I know that
   I am, but I don't need to hear it over and over.
   I can see in people's eyes that they are uncomfortable when I get a little hyper. I can
   also see when they think I'm acting weird. It
   hurts, and I wish that I could explain why I
   act differently but it's too hard, and no one
   really cares sometimes.

2. **What do you think that ASD is for you? How
   do you think it makes you different?**
   It makes me a little more hyper than others. I'm a very competitive person and hate
   to lose; that's also a part of it. I feel like I always need to find that right person to hang
   around with. I need to find people that get
   me. It's also hard for me to change subjects
   in a conversation. Sometimes I can see that
   people are tired with what I'm talking about,
   but I have to get it off my chest or all out of
   my head before I can stop. Most of the time,
   I don't see when people are irritated. I also
   don't know if I'm offending someone because
   I can't tell by looking at them. A lot of people

think that I mean to be rude, but I don't. I'm just trying to fit in. If I say something that sounds rude, the best thing to do is tell me; then I'll know. But people assume a lot when it comes to how I act. That hurts.

3. **Do you ever wish that you didn't have ASD, and why?**

That's tough. Sometimes yes and sometimes no. I like being different from everyone else, and there are some perks. At most amusement parks, I get to go to the front of the line, and I know that I wouldn't get that if it weren't for ASD. I also have a great memory and sense of humor that I think is from ASD. But sometimes I feel like ASD is the reason that I don't have many friends. I think it's the reason why no one seems to understand me. I want to be calm, but inside, either my brain will just fix on one thing, or my nerves will be jumping around. It's like I can't always control it. I wish that I had a controller that could make me calm when I want to be calm and hyper when I want to be fun.

4. **How would your life be different if you didn't have ASD?**

I can't really tell. No ADA passes at amusement parks! People would treat me differently. I wouldn't be bullied so much, I think.

In school, I'm in the middle group, some-where between the athlete group and nerds. If I didn't have ASD, I would probably have to pick a side, and I wouldn't like that. But I think I would have more friends, and I think that I might be happier more of the time.

5. **What do you want people to know about you?**
   I want them to know that I'm different and I'm proud of that. Everyone is unique in [his or her] own way, and that's OK. No matter what, and no matter how down you get, you should be happy that you're not like every-one else. What is normal, anyway? I also wish that teachers would understand that every-one has different needs. I want teachers to listen to me and to try to understand where I'm coming from. That's been hard. We all start out as perfect pegs. Then life gives you dents, and it shapes us so that we're all differ-ent. So please don't try to put me in a round hole. I'm kind of square.

6. **What is your dream job?**
   Anything to do with cars. That's my passion. I think I would be a good Hot Wheels car de-signer. I want to work on my computer in my PJs and eat chips all day. I wouldn't mind designing real cars, either. I think I'd like to visit other countries and definitely drive on the autobahn.

Alexander

1. **Can you tell that Jackie has ASD?**

   Most of the time, no. I can go months at a time without remembering. I'm used to him. Then I see moments of extreme anger and remember that he has a hard time controlling himself. I don't feel afraid, and I think it's important for him to let it out. It's still loud, and that's the thing that bothers me. But then his anger is over quickly, and it's back to normal, whatever that is.

2. **What are some things that make him different from other friends?**

   The lack of a filter is something that can be challenging. He can say things that seem strange or weird or are not appropriate. Most people can't understand this, and [so] he comes off looking mean or immature. The hyperactivity is also different. He can't calm down, and he gets in your face sometimes. I can see how other people might be afraid of that.

3. **What do you have in common with Jackie?**

   Jackie and I both see the world differently, in an abstract way. I think we both feel like we're not like the other kids and don't really fit into normal social cliques. Both of us are OK with that. There's no reason to have labels on anyone. We both believe in being who we are. And, of course, we both like technology and cars.

4. **What makes you frustrated in dealing with Jackie and his ASD?**

   The most frustrating thing is watching him trying to fit in. Sometimes it doesn't work, and it's sad to see it happen. It's like he's trying too hard, and then he thinks that what he's saying is making him a part of the group, but [it's] not really. Sometimes his ideas don't fit into what we're talking about. It's not his fault at all. Sometimes I wish that friends could just accept him.

Autism Spectrum Disorder is a rough and rocky road to travel. Even with all the stress, drama, and frustration, I try to celebrate who Jackie is as well as all of his accomplishments. The chess trophies line his bedroom shelves, the National Junior Honor Society awards hang on the wall, and the Science Olympiad medals rest on his desk, all reminders of what there is to celebrate. But the celebration is more than just tangible awards; it's so much more. It's a celebration of the endeavor to understand ourselves and to share that in a positive way with the world.

 Diane Mayer Christiansen is a published author writing young adult fantasy and middle school chapter books. Her characters are based on children with special needs such as dyslexia and Autism Spectrum Disorder. She speaks to parents and teachers about learning to celebrate those things that make our children different and her journey with her son and his ASD.

Jackie and Alexander

CPSIA information can be obtained
at www.ICGtesting.com
Printed in the USA
LVOW01s1749030517
533132LV00010B/1166/P